Beginner's Guide To Starting a YouTube Channel: 2024-2025 Edition

How To Become a Social Media Influencer & Content Creator

By Ann Eckhart

INTRODUCTION

Do you love to watch YouTube videos? Do you want to start your own channel but have no idea where to start?

Then this is the book for you!

For years, I have been teaching people how easy it is to start a YouTube channel for both fun and profit. In this, my latest guidebook, I will walk you step-by-step through the entire process along with the latest updates from the site.

But first, let me share with you my journey to becoming a YouTube content creator.

I began my YouTube journey in 2001. I was five years into running a home-based reselling business where I sold wholesale gift items on eBay and Amazon. I had outgrown my townhome, and with an elderly father and two dogs in my household, I needed more space. I'd just purchased a new home and was settling into my new basement workspace when my sales started to dip.

I had been early to the online selling game. When I first started selling on eBay, eBay was the only shopping site that allowed third-party sellers. In fact, eBay was pretty much the only website that sold anything besides books. If you are old enough to remember, Amazon initially started as an online bookstore. It took them several years before they started to sell anything other than media.

For those of us who were the first to sell online, there was virtually no competition anywhere on the world wide web. eBay was not just "the" place to sell; it was the "only" place to sell. Sales came in fast and steady with little effort other than getting a listing up and then shipping it out. My business was, I have to admit, pretty easy to run. I sold on eBay exclusively for nearly two years before expanding to Amazon when they opened their site to third-party sellers through their Merchant Fulfilled program.

My Amazon sales took off leaving eBay in the dust, and I had phenomenal growth every year It seemed as if the possibilities were endless to grow my business and make more money.

However, that was until the year the floor fell out from under me. That was the year the rest of the retail community started to catch up, starting their own e-commerce websites and beginning to sell on eBay and Amazon. For me, that year came just as I'd purchased my new home with an entire space dedicated to online selling. But now what was I supposed to sell?

Not only were other people starting to sell the same items that I was, but the wholesale companies I bought from were also starting to sell directly to customers online, too. After years of no competition, I was suddenly surrounded by competitors who were undercutting my prices and offering perks I could not afford, such as free shipping. Seemingly overnight, I could no longer stay competitive, and my business seemed doomed.

But then I stumbled upon YouTube. And through YouTube, my business was given a new life. In fact, YouTube, specifically those YouTube creators who were posting videos, saved my business.

I had never watched a YouTube video before that fateful day when I did an internet search about selling on eBay. I'd heard about YouTube, of course, but had never even thought to log on. However, I began searching online hoping to find a book or website to help me figure out what to do with my business. I desperately needed a magic bullet to help me salvage what I had worked so hard to build.

So, imagine my surprise when my search results revealed several YouTube videos with titles such as "What I sold on eBay from garage sales" and "How I make money selling used clothing from thrift stores." Intrigued, I followed the links and found a small group of people who called themselves "pickers."

These "pickers," or "resellers," as most people now call them, were making videos on YouTube about their thriving eBay businesses. And not one of them was buying new items wholesale the way I had been! While buying brand new items was easy for me to order and list, these sellers, who ran their businesses from their homes, were earning more money than I ever had and they were doing it by sourcing secondhand items.

I quickly became immersed in the videos these "pickers" were sharing about how they were selling garage sale and thrift store finds on eBay. While I had always known that there were antique dealers who sold at antique stores and flea markets, I somehow never made the connection that these same vintage items could be sold on eBay. I saw antiques as a specialized skill set, one I knew nothing about. But I soon learned that "antiques" were just the tip of the iceberg when it came to finding items to resell. And I quickly saw how I, too, could sell used items online, replacing my wholesale gifts and making me more money than ever before.

My business, which I had thought was over, suddenly got a new life as I learned all about reselling. While it was hard to give up the ease of ordering new items directly from the manufacturer (complete with photos and measurements), I was desperate to avoid returning to working for someone else. So, I hunkered down and learned all that I could.

It took a lot of trial and error, but I successfully transitioned my business from selling new gift products to selling thrifted finds. I started scouring estate sales for vintage collectibles and went to half-off days at the thrift store to buy clothing to resell. I gave up selling on Amazon and refocused my efforts solely on eBay, liquidating my remaining wholesale inventory and listing everything from vintage collectibles to electronics.

This new business model saved my business, and it was thanks to the people in the "picking community" who were making videos on YouTube. Those YouTube creators and the YouTube site itself not only saved my business but learning how to resell secondhand items eventually led me to write books such as the one you are currently reading!

From having an online gift shop to reselling secondhand items to becoming a full-time author. It's been a wild two decades of self-employment! And in between those business adventures, I also started making YouTube videos.

When I first started watching YouTube videos, I had no intention of starting my own channel. Rather, I interacted with the video creators by leaving comments on their uploads and formed friendships that last to this day. It was fun to talk to other eBay sellers, and we happily shared information, celebrating our successes and encouraging each other when things weren't going well.

However, they also all encouraged me to start my own YouTube channel. But I was terrified to upload my own videos. Not only did I hate public speaking and being on camera, but I also had no idea how to start a YouTube channel.

Eventually, though, I got up the courage and took the leap to start my own channel. With some help from my YouTube friends, I finally figured out how to film and upload videos.

But my first YouTube videos were terrible! I used an old iPhone (I think it was an iPhone 4), and since I initially filmed in my basement office, the lighting was awful, which made my videos dark. I constantly forgot to look at the camera, and I had to remind myself to speak up to be heard. And don't even get me started on my unflattering camera angle. All in all, my first YouTube videos were a mess!

I honestly wanted to quit YouTube shortly after I started. But with the encouragement of my "picking" friends, I kept going, slowly gaining confidence in my filming abilities. And I also started growing an audience.

I would gladly give you the URL to my first channel so you could see how bad my videos were, except that it no longer exists. Why? Well, back when I first started on YouTube, you could sign up for a channel using any email address, so I used the one that came with my internet provider. However, when Google introduced monetization, you could only monetize your channel if you signed up using a Gmail account, the email that Google provides.

The bottom line was that I had built an audience on a channel I could not make money on. So, I had to start a brand-new channel using a Google account and began the long process of rebuilding my audience.

Don't worry: You will not have to face this same issue. Today the only way to start a YouTube channel is when you sign up with a Google Gmail account.

It took a while for me to move my audience from my old channel to my new one, but once I had, I deleted my original channel and focused on my new channel. Honestly, it was nice to start fresh as I was more comfortable on camera and had upped my production value. I'm also glad those old videos aren't around to haunt me (I told you they were bad, and I meant it!)

However, the best part of my new channel was that I was finally earning money from my videos with Google AdSense. There are many ways to earn money on YouTube, and the first is with Google AdSense. Google owns YouTube and sells advertising that runs before, during, and after videos. Google shares this advertising revenue with YouTube creators.

I didn't earn much money to start, maybe a couple of hundred dollars a month. But I loved making videos and being part of the YouTube "reselling community." For me, YouTube was fun. I was not only making friends, but I was learning so much about business. And the extra money was a nice bonus.

After a few years with just one channel, I started a second channel. Why start a second channel when I already had a successful one? Well, it was because I wanted to upload different content. While my first channel focused solely on my eBay business, I initially started my second channel to focus on my Walt Disney World vacation vlogs. At the time, I anticipated going down to Orlando, Florida, twice a year and filming lots of videos for that channel.

However, life happened, and I became a full-time caregiver for my elderly father. Not only were vacations out of the question, but full-time reselling had to take a backseat as it required too much time and effort. I needed to streamline all my businesses, and that included YouTube.

Figuring out what to do with my YouTube channels took me on a roller coaster of a journey with attempts at various content. I tried lifestyle vlogs and subscription box reviews; I even had a short-lived podcast-style show called "The Reselling Report." I felt like I was spinning in a million directions, trying to find something that worked. At one point, even after building an online following, I almost gave up on YouTube as I was at a loss as to what content to provide.

But giving up YouTube was harder than sticking with it. After all, I had spent years growing my channels. Eventually, I had to take an "I can only do what I can do" attitude regarding what types of videos I could film and which channel to put them on. At the end of the day, I reminded myself that I had started making YouTube videos for fun. Sure, the extra money was nice. But I needed to enjoy myself if I was going to continue producing content.

Today, I have one active YouTube channel, "Ann Eckhart." I vlog three times a week, covering everything from my various businesses (I still sell on eBay but also have two Etsy shops along with my publishing business) to lifestyle content that includes my life in Iowa and my pug dogs.

As I said earlier, my YouTube journey has been a roller coaster. There have been times when I was consistently earning over $1,200 a month from my videos and other times when I had to take a break from filming, which plummeted my earnings. I have changed my content and upload schedule more times than I can count, and my channels have suffered for it as YouTube favors consistency.

Today, however, I have found a happy medium for being a YouTuber. As I said, I now film vlogs three times a week and focus on a single channel. I still have a good group of friends I've made on YouTube, and I still love to watch other YouTube channels. YouTube is part of my daily routine, and I can't see that changing any time soon.

Fortunately for you, in this book, you will be learning from all my mistakes, which will help you succeed with your channel right out of the gate. From setting up your account and learning how to upload videos to building your brand and earning money, I'll be teaching you all of the ins and outs of YouTube that I've mastered over the years.

This book may be titled *Beginner's Guide To Starting a YouTube Channel,* but in fact, it is the ultimate guide to help you not only start a channel but also grow it. With just a computer, camera, and internet access, anyone can start a YouTube channel. But it takes work and perseverance to grow a channel and earn money from it.

Whether you have yet to start your YouTube channel or have already begun posting videos, I guarantee this book has something to help you get started and start making money!

FUN FACTS:

◇ YouTube has more than 2.70 BILLION active users

◇ 52% of internet users access YouTube at least once a month

◇ Over 122 million people visit YouTube every day via the web or apps.

◇ 720,000 hours of video are uploaded to YouTube every day.

◇ Mr. Beast is the highest-earning YouTuber who earned $54 million in 2022.

◇ Users consume 1 billion hours of videos on YouTube every day.

◇ The majority of YouTube users are between the age of 25-34.

◇ Comedy is the most-watched genre on YouTube.

◈ YouTube removed the dislike button from the platform in 2021. Before removing the dislike button, YouTube's Rewind for 2018 was the most disliked video of all time, with 20.8 million dislikes.

CHAPTER ONE: SIGNING UP FOR A YOUTUBE CHANNEL

YouTube was founded nearly two decades ago by three PayPal employees: Chad Hurley, Steve Chen, and Jawed Karin. PayPal, if you remember, was eBay's original payment processing system. How funny is it that the men who would start YouTube initially worked for PayPal, the payment service I initially relied on to run my eBay business? It's a small tech world, indeed!

According to internet lore, Hurley, Chen, and Karin started YouTube in a small space above a Japanese restaurant and a pizzeria in San Mateo, California. Sounds a bit like how Steve Jobs and Steve Wozniak started Apple in a California garage, doesn't it? It was Karin who was the star of the first video ever uploaded to YouTube: "Me at the Zoo." It was only a shaky 19-second-long clip, but it would revolutionize the internet space forever.

Hurley, Chen, and Karin activated the domain name "YouTube.com" on February 14, 2005, with the original concept of it being an online dating series. However, when that idea failed due to a lack of users, the young entrepreneurs focused on making YouTube a place for non-computer experts to publish, upload, and stream videos through standard web browsers and household modems. Initially, video clips were limited to 100 megabytes with as little as 30 seconds of footage. Views grew to around 30,000 per day within months with only 10 employees working behind the scenes

Everything changed a year later when Google purchased YouTube in 2006 for $1.65 billion in stock, making the three young founders instant millionaires. After Google purchased YouTube, the site rapidly grew, reaching 43% of the video market by the end of 2010. In the next few years, much was done to make YouTube more accessible to small content creators while also building the company up, including adding AdSense advertising payments for creators. Now people can upload videos not only for fun but also for profit.

Over the years, YouTube has grown from a small niche website to a platform with nearly three billion users worldwide. Today, creators, both large and small, produce videos, both for entertainment purchases as well as for business, for users across the globe. And with nearly 122 million viewers logging onto the site every day, YouTube has shown no signs of slowing down, continuing to grow yearly.

Needless to say, YouTube has become a part of everyday life for a large population of people across the globe. With content ranging from cooking, crafting, traveling, and family vlogging to gaming, beauty, style, news, comedy, finance, and business, there is something for everyone to watch on YouTube. And there is always a ready audience of YouTube viewers searching for new videos.

So, you may be wondering, is there a place for YOU on this overcrowded site? The answer is YES! Anyone can start a YouTube channel today and work to make it successful. The key is that you must start your channel! And the sooner, the better!

I won't lie to you, however. YouTube is a much more competitive space than even just a few years ago. New creators are continually joining the site, and videos' production value is lightyears ahead of where they were initially. Gone are the days when you could build a large following with a shaky old smartphone in a dimly lit room.

To build a successful and profitable channel, you need to be committed to filming good, consistent content. Fortunately, the actual process of filming and uploading videos is the easy part. With smartphone technology, it's possible to film, edit, and upload videos right from your phone, bypassing expensive cameras and editing software. But once your video is uploaded, you will need to work on marketing your channel and handling back-end work. Filming is the easy part of YouTube; it's the other work that takes most of a creator's time.

YouTube makes it easy to upload videos, but it is Google that will pay you to do it. YouTube creators can make money on the site because Google owns the actual website itself. Google enabled channels to start making money from their videos in 2008. The rate they pay varies by the type of ads that run on the videos, but everyone is paid per 1,000 views. Some people make 50 cents per 1,000 views, while others earn hundreds.

Not only has this partnership between YouTube and Google been beneficial for channel creators, but it has also proved to be a lucrative opportunity for advertisers as they can reach customers across the globe for a fraction of the cost of television advertising. Think about it: Don't you see a lot of companies advertising on YouTube that you have never seen advertise on television? Google has given small companies a way to reach way more customers than if they were just running ads on TV.

However, it isn't just Google that will pay you to make videos. Brand sponsorships are another way creators can earn income on YouTube. Some creators earn more from sponsorships than they do from AdSense! There are also channel memberships available where viewers pay a monthly fee for additional content. While most people, such as myself, look at YouTube as a way to bring in some additional income, other people have made YouTube their full-time job.

YouTube currently runs ads on over a billion video views every week, giving a cut of the advertising revenue to creators. I will be talking in-depth about making money from your videos from AdSense, sponsorships, and other ways later in this book. But before you can make any money, you must properly set up your YouTube and Google accounts.

Since Google owns YouTube and controls the AdSense advertising that pays you for your videos, **you must first sign up with Google to create a YouTube channel** that will earn you ad revenue.

As I talked about in the *Introduction* to this book, when I started my first YouTube channel, I didn't do it through Google but instead registered through a non-Google email account. Because I did not sign up for my first YouTube channel through a Google email address, that initial channel could not be monetized. Despite consistently uploading videos and building an audience, I never earned a penny from those videos.

Fortunately, you do not have to worry about making the same mistake I made because today, you can only get a YouTube channel through Google. You can skip this next section if you already have a Gmail account through Google. But if you do not have a Gmail email address, it is free and easy to set one up. Here is how:

GOOGLE ACCOUNT: To sign up for a Google account that will allow you to create a YouTube account (from which you can like, comment, and subscribe to videos) and a YouTube channel (where you can upload your own videos), head to the Google Account sign-up page at **accounts.google.com/signup**. The registration process is quick, easy, and completely free.

The Google account page will allow you to create a **Google account**, a **YouTube account**, a **Google "@gmail.com" email address**, and a **YouTube channel**, all in one place.

Simply follow the online prompts to complete the process. A Google account will first give you your own YouTube account, which will enable you to interact with other creators' content (such as subscribing to channels, giving videos a "thumbs up", and leaving comments). If you've been watching YouTube videos before this, you may have noticed the inability to leave comments on videos, as this is only available to those with a YouTube account.

In addition to giving you your own YouTube account, Google will also give you your own YouTube channel. However, it is up to you if you want to activate your channel. Once you have created a YouTube account, you can click on your username and see that a channel has already been created for you.

Many people with YouTube accounts never create their channels, but the option is already built-in once you have an account. You will be prompted to create your channel by Google; the process is as simple as naming your channel. Don't worry if you are not ready to upload anything right away; the creation of your channel simply means that it is there if and when you are ready.

CHANNEL NAME: When you create your Google account, you will choose a username. Most people make this their actual name, and, unless you already have a business or brand, I recommend that. You can then choose a different name for your actual YouTube channel. Your Google username is different from your YouTube channel name.

Be sure to choose your YouTube channel name wisely. Google usually prompts you to make it the same as your account name, but you can select any name you like, just as long as another account is not currently using it. While you may just be starting on YouTube for fun now, you do not want to limit yourself from growing your brand in the future. Many established, successful YouTube channels have names unrelated to their content because the people behind them never anticipated how large their channels would grow.

And while you can change your channel name if you decide to later on, it can confuse your subscribers. I named my first YouTube channel, the one that is no longer active, the same as my eBay store name, the name under which my reselling business was registered. Since I was only creating eBay content at the time, that name made sense.

However, shortly afterward, I started a now-defunct blog called "SeeAnnSave," where I posted about couponing and free samples. It was at this same time that I started my second YouTube channel using a Google account so that I could earn AdSense on my videos. Once I realized that keeping that first channel wasn't financially worth it, I decided to delete that channel and named my new YouTube channel "SeeAnnSave" to match my blog, as I wanted to post money-saving videos in addition to my reselling content. Most of my followers on YouTube today subscribed to my channel when it was "SeeAnnSave" and some still call it that to this day.

After several years, I closed my blog and changed my channel name to my name, "Ann Eckhart." Since I publish books under my own name, it made the most sense to "brand" all of my content under the same name, YouTube included. I also changed my social media handles to match. "SeeAnnSave" became "Ann Eckhart" on YouTube, Facebook, Twitter, and Instagram.

While Google allowed me to make the name change, I had to completely rebrand everything, including my channel artwork and logos. Plus, I had to change the names of all my social media accounts. It was a considerable undertaking, and while it was worth it in the long run, it took a lot of work. Plus, for quite a long time, I had to continually explain to my subscribers why the name was different.

If I had to do it all over again, I would have stuck with naming my channel my name the way it is now!

And as I mentioned, some people still refer to me as "SeeAnnSave." So, while you are not locked into the first name you choose, note that it is better to get it right the first time to save yourself the headache of changing everything later on. And if you cannot come up with anything unique, it is perfectly fine to use your real name. In fact, many YouTube creators who started with quirky channel names later changed them to their real names.

Note that after you change your channel name, you can also **change the URL address at youtube.com/handle.**

If you plan to make your YouTube channel your main website, you may want to purchase a dedicated URL from a site such as GoDaddy.com and have it directed to your channel. For instance, I own the URL AnnEckhart.com, which I have set to direct users to my Amazon Author Page automatically. My books are my primary source of income, and I want people to visit my author page above all of my other websites. However, I would point the URL directly to my channel if YouTube was my full-time job.

Owning the URLs to your channel name is a good idea in the long run. While you may start your channel just for fun, it may grow to the point where you want to "brand" your content. And if your Google AdSense grows significantly, you will want to be able to quickly direct people to your channel, which is much easier with a dedicated URL. Plus, you want to secure your URL name before someone else buys it.

URLs are inexpensive to obtain and are something you will want to investigate as your channel grows. Choosing the ".com" version is the most logical, but if your channel becomes large, you will want to secure all the domains (.org, .net, etc.). And if your channel name is different from your own name, you may want to own the URLs for your name, too. I still own the "SeeAnnSave" URLs, the URLs for my legal name, the URLs for my eBay store, my Etsy shops, and additional pen names.

CHAPTER TWO: REGISTERING FOR A GOOGLE ADSENSE ACCOUNT

Since Google owns YouTube, it makes money by selling advertising on the site, specifically ads that are played before, during, and after videos. Creators can earn a cut of this ad revenue through the YouTube Partner Program. Google's ad program is called **Google AdSense**. Registering for a Google AdSense account is a separate process from creating a YouTube channel.

Channels must meet certain milestones before their videos can be monetized. However, you can sign up for a Google AdSense account even before you are eligible, which you want to do so that when you qualify, you will be ready to start earning money on your videos.

While you used to start earning AdSense money right out of the gate on YouTube, in 2019, Google changed the requirements for becoming monetized (i.e., allowing you to place ads on your videos to earn a cut of the revenue from them). Now a channel needs to have 1,000 subscribers AND 4,000 hours of views within 12 months before it can start making AdSense money. Or, if a channel has 1,000 subscribers and 10 million valid public Shorts views within 90 days, it can also become monetized.

YouTube Shorts are video clips that are 60 seconds or less. They were added to the site to compete with TikTok and Instagram Reels. Many large TikTok creators now upload their TikTok to YouTube as Shorts and earn money without making full-length videos.

Note that YouTube is now taking AdSense away from inactive channels and making creators re-earn their monetization by getting back up to 4,000 watch hours within a year. So, if you were once monetized but haven't been posting videos, you may need to start uploading again to qualify.

While these new requirements are frustrating for new YouTube creators and also to YouTube creators who may have stepped away from their channels for a bit and lost their AdSense, you can get your channel to monetization standards rather quickly with dedication and consistency. I will go over ways to grow your channel later in this book. But first, more about AdSense.

According to Google, AdSense works in three steps:

1. You make your ad spaces available by pasting ad codes on your blog or website and placing ads on your YouTube videos.
2. The highest-paying ads appear on your site as advertisers bid to show in your ad spaces in real-time auctions.
3. Creators are paid directly by Google, with Google handling the process of billing all advertisers for the ads that show up on your content.

As part of the AdSense Program, Google delivers ads to your blog, website, and/or YouTube channel via their Google Ads system. Google then pays you for the advertisements displayed on your videos based on user clicks on ads OR ad impressions, depending on the ad type.

Creators cannot choose the ads that appear on their sites/videos. Advertisers tell Google the content they want their ads targeted on, not the other way around. Tech companies are willing to spend more on ads than, say, beauty products. And come election time, all bets are off as campaign ads flood the site. Despite your political views, you cannot control an ad from a candidate you don't support from placing ads on your videos.

Google uses three methods to determine which ads are placed; according to them, these are:

1. **Contextual Targeting:** Google technology uses factors such as keyword analysis, word frequency, font size, and the overall link structure of the internet to determine what a site or video is about and precisely how to match Google ads to that particular content.

2. **Placement Targeting:** Under this format, advertisers can choose specific ad placements to run their ads. Ads that are placement-targeted may not be precisely related to a page's content but are instead hand-selected by advertisers who have decided that there is a match between the products/services and what your readers/viewers are interested in.

3. **Personalized Targeting:** This offering enables advertisers to reach users based on their interests, demographics, the types of websites they visit, the apps on their mobile devices, the cookies on their web browsers, the activity on their devices, previous interactions with other Google ads, and their own Google Account activity and information.

CREATE AN ADSENSE ACCOUNT: To monetize your videos, you will first need to become a YouTube Partner, which we will discuss in the next section of this chapter. As I mentioned, you now must have 1,000 subscribers and 4,000 hours of watch time before you can monetize your videos. However, if you have a blog or website, you will want to go ahead and sign up for a Google AdSense account now, as you can start earning money from ads on websites immediately. There is no threshold you need to meet to make money from Google ads on a website. I was earning Google AdSense on my blog a couple of months before I started making money on my videos.

Simply visit **google.com/adsense/start** to begin the application process. Note that you will need to go through a verification process to qualify for an account, including providing your **social security number** for tax purposes and your **bank routing information** for direct deposit of your earnings. Some people are wary of providing this information, but it is the same as you would do if you were applying for a job. If you expect Google to pay you, they will need your information for tax purposes. Google sends you a 1099 tax form if you make money from ads within a calendar year.

Note that once you are monetized and have $10 in your account, Google will send you a PIN code via mail or email that you will need to provide to complete the application process. The process changes every so often, but Google will provide you with all the instructions to follow when submitting your application.

AdSense earnings are paid via direct deposit to your bank account. You must reach $100 in total AdSense earnings across all platforms (blog/website/YouTube) to receive a monthly payout. For years, I had AdSense on both my blog and YouTube, so I easily met that $100 monthly threshold every month. If you don't meet the $100 payout minimum in a month, the amount will carry over into the following months until you reach $100. Once you earn the money, you can't lose it; you just may have to wait until they release it to you.

In late 2021, I shut my blog down and now only earn AdSense through YouTube. My payout is automatically deposited into my bank account around the third week of the month.

Since AdSense is income, you do have to pay taxes on the money you earn. Fortunately, Google makes it easy by sending users tax forms every year. You can have your Google 1099 form mailed to you, or you can download it from your account. Do not worry about missing it: Google will notify you when the forms are available. If you don't get a notification, you simply log into your Google AdSense account, and you will find your tax form there to print.

While AdSense is usually the most significant chunk of income for most channels, you must also keep track of any sponsorship or affiliate money you receive. Not all companies will send out tax forms for brand deals or affiliate advertising income. I have several affiliate marketing partnerships that never send out tax forms, but I still keep track of the money they pay me. I will discuss these additional forms of income and managing your YouTube finances later in this book.

Once you have completed the application process and have been approved for an AdSense account, you can begin placing AdSense ads on your blog or website. However, you will have to wait to be eligible to join the **YouTube Partner Program** to start monetizing your YouTube videos. You cannot join the program until you reach 1,000 subscribers and 4,000 watch hours. Your channel won't automatically be monetized when you reach these goals. Joining the YouTube Partner Program is an additional step you will need to complete; do not worry, as Google will prompt you to do it once your channel is eligible.

BECOMING A YOUTUBE PARTNER: After you have created your Google account, YouTube channel, and AdSense account, there is one more step you will need to take before you can start earning money on your videos, and that is to become a **YouTube Partner**.

Once your channel reaches 1,000 subscribers and 4,000 watch hours, YouTube will prompt you to sign up with their YouTube Partner Program.

According to YouTube, *The YouTube Partner Program (YPP) gives creators greater access to YouTube resources and features,"* including access to *YouTube's creator support teams, copyright match tools, and monetization features.*

The minimum eligibility requirements to join the YouTube Partner Program include:

- Following all the current YouTube monetization policies (these are frequently updated; once you are going through the application process, you will be prompted to agree to them)
- Live in a country or region where the YPP is available
- Have 1,000 channel subscribers and 4,000 valid public watch hours within 12 months
- OR have 1,000 channel subscribers and 10 million valid public watch hours on SHORTS within 90 days
- Have a linked AdSense account (again, this is an excellent reason to create your AdSense account even before you are eligible to apply to be a YouTube Partner, as you will be ready to go once you meet the requirements)

Here is an abbreviated *YouTube Partner Program* application checklist:

1. Make sure your channel follows all policies and guidelines. You will go through a standard review process when you apply to check if your channel meets these standards.
2. Enable 2-Step Verification for your Google account, which means you will protect your account with both your password and an additional device.
3. Have 1,000 channel subscribers and 4,000 valid public watch hours within 12 months
4. OR have 1,000 channel subscribers and 10 million valid public watch hours on SHORTS within 90 days
5. Sign YTP terms to be notified when you are eligible to apply to become a YouTube Partner. You can do this manually, although YouTube will prompt you once you meet the subscriber and view thresholds.

6. Make sure you only have ONE AdSense account (you cannot have multiple accounts under your name).

7. Once you sign the YouTube Partner Program terms and connect your AdSense account, your channel will be put into a queue for review. Both automated systems and human reviewers will then review your channel's content before being accepted into the YouTube Partner Program. Note that it can take up to a month for your account to be reviewed; it depends on how many other accounts are in line before you and how much staff is currently available to conduct reviews.

MONETIZING YOUR VIDEOS: Your videos must be monetized for them to start earning income. Monetization means you authorize YouTube to place ads in your videos and agree that no copyrighted materials (music and video clips from TV shows, movies, or other licensed sources) appear in your footage.

If a piece of music accidentally makes it through, YouTube will likely still allow the video to play BUT will not allow ads to be placed on it, meaning you will not make any money from that particular video. These music copyright strikes happened to me frequently when I was vlogging my Walt Disney World vacations, as much of the music played inside the parks was copyrighted. Fortunately, while I could not earn AdSense on those videos, YouTube allowed them to remain on their site. While I could have edited the music out, I chose to keep it in so that I could enjoy it when I watched the videos back myself.

In some cases, the music copyright allows you to make money from the parts of the video that do NOT contain the copyrighted music, which still allows you to make money from the rest of your video.

Avoiding copyrighted music is a big reason why many vloggers do voice-overs on their footage. Many stores play music that, if picked up by your camera's microphone, will trigger YouTube to de-monetize your video. Do not worry if this happens; it will not negatively affect your other videos or prevent you from uploading again. It just means that the particular video, or parts of it, will not earn you any AdSense.

If you upload a video that triggers YouTube's copyright system, you can always delete it and re-edit the footage to take the music clips out. If only a small part of your video contains copyrighted music, YouTube can narrow it down for you, and you can choose to have them edit it out for you. This process can take a while, but it is often easier than editing your original footage and reuploading it. Once you have been filming for a while, you will learn where and when to avoid vlogging to prevent copyright issues.

An AdSense account does not automatically mean your videos will earn money, as **you need to monetize each of your videos manually**. This is done in the **YouTube Studio** section of your YouTube account.

You can access your YouTube Studio on your desktop computer or via the YouTube Studio app. Note that the YouTube Studio app is separate from the YouTube app. While I have the YouTube Studio app downloaded on my phone, I prefer to use the YouTube Studio section on my computer as it is easier to access and edit all available features.

The following directions are based on using YouTube Studio on a computer, not in the app:

Once a video is uploaded to your YouTube channel, go to your **YouTube Studio**. This section is accessible by clicking on your profile picture in the top right-hand corner of your YouTube account.

Click on **Content** to access your videos.

Find the video you want to monetize and click on the **edit icon** (it looks like a pencil) that will appear when you hover your mouse under the video title.

A new page titled **Video details** will open.

Click on the **$ Monetization tab** on the left-hand side of the page. You can monetize your videos through the *YouTube Studio* app, but there are more options on the desktop version.

Clicking on the **$ Monetization** tab will bring up the **Video Monetization** page of your chosen video.

Select **On** from the **Monetization drop-down menu**. The **Type of ads section** will now be accessible for you to select. If your video is over eight minutes long, you will be able to select from the following (or choose all of them):

- **Display ads:** This is the default option that indicates that Google will be placing ads on your videos.
- **Overlay ads:** Overlay image or text ads that can appear on the lower 20% portion of a video. These types of ads appear on videos viewed from a computer, not on mobile or other devices.
- **Sponsored cards:** Sponsored cards are very small call-to-action pop-ups that creators can add to their videos that will take them to past videos they reference or a link to another page the creator wants viewers to visit. These are used mainly for sponsored content.
- **Skippable video ads:** Skippable video ads allow viewers to skip ads after they have been running for 5 sections.
- **Non-skippable video ads:** Non-skippable video ads must be watched before a video can be viewed.

Under the **Type of ads** section is the **Location of video ads** section. Here is where you can choose where ads will be placed in your videos, including:

- **Before video** (pre-roll)
- **During video** (mid-roll)
- **After video** (post-roll)

If your video is over eight minutes long, you will also want to click on the **MANAGE MID-ROLL** option found under **During video (mid-roll).** The advertisements that run in the middle of videos typically bring in the most revenue, so you will want to ensure they are placed effectively in your videos.

YouTube will automatically place mid-roll ads for you as a default option, but I like to make my own selections to ensure that the ads are not too close together. Sometimes YouTube will put in way too many ads or put all the ads right together, which will turn viewers off. Or sometimes they may not put enough ads in. Google also tends to insert ads into strange places within videos, such as at the very end of the video when viewers have already clicked off and are no longer watching.

Depending on the video's length, I typically place my ads every seven to ten minutes. For instance, I will place ads for a fifteen-minute video at the seven-minute mark. If a video is twenty-five minutes long, I might place ads at nine and nineteen minutes.

Placing ad breaks is easy; you simply **click on the "+" next to AD BREAK** and click to add as many individual placements as you want. Then, under the **PLACE AUTOMATICALLY** column, you enter the time stamp for each. You can easily change these, so do not worry about making a mistake.

You can also manually move each ad break to the end of the video. I will walk you through the step-by-step process I personally go through to monetize my videos later in this book.

Once you have your ad breaks where you want them, simply click on the **SAVE** button in the top right corner to confirm your selections.

A pop-up box will appear on your screen titled **Tell us what's in your video**. Here you will need to confirm whether your video contains **Inappropriate language, Adult content, Violence, Shocking content, Harmful or dangerous acts, Drug-related content, Hateful Content, Firearms-related content**, and/or **Sensitive issues.** YouTube strictly controls videos that contain any of those types of content, so unless your videos contain any of them, you will simply check **None of the above** before hitting the **Submit** button.

Click **SAVE** again, and you will be done with monetizing your videos!

Make sure to go back into your old videos, the ones that were not monetized initially, to monetize them, too. The mid-roll ads are especially important, so even though it can be time-consuming to update your older videos with them, it will be worth it in terms of your earnings.

Note that I will be going into more detail about how I upload, edit, and prepare my videos in *Chapter Ten: A Day in the Life of a YouTuber* to give you a better idea about managing your own uploads.

The steps to set up and monetize your YouTube channel can seem overwhelming for new creators. Signing up for a Google account, an AdSense account, and a YouTube account, plus applying for the YouTube Partner Program, all take time. You need to ensure that the information you provide is accurate; after all, you are asking that Google pay you for ads placed in and on your content. It is almost like applying for a job, plus you also need to make sure your tax information is correct.

Be patient, and make sure to follow all the instructions when you are filling out your applications. While signing up for a Google account and YouTube channel is automatic once you have submitted the forms, being accepted into the YouTube Partner Program can take a bit of time depending on how many other people are applying, as Google employees manually verify each account. Sometimes it only takes a week for accounts to be verified; other times, it takes a few months. The wait can be frustrating, but once you are monetized and start earning money from your videos, I promise it will be worth it.

And remember that you only must do these tasks once. After you have all your accounts set up and have monetized your YouTube videos, you will be able to relax and enjoy the monthly deposits of money into your bank account!

CHAPTER THREE: BEST CAMERAS FOR FILMING VIDEOS

When beginning any new venture, I believe it is always best to start with what you already have before investing in anything new. This chapter will cover the types of products needed to film, edit, and upload YouTube videos, along with examples of the current top products being used by creators. While I cannot tell you the exact setup to use, you will come away with the knowledge of what is out there and can then decide if you want to purchase any of it or if you can make do with what you already own.

As I've already mentioned, I do all my filming, editing, and uploading on my iPhone. In fact, I have only ever produced my YouTube videos using an iPhone. While I use apps to edit and upload my videos, I use my laptop to complete the back-end production aspects for my channel. In the chapter *A Day In The Life Of A Youtuber,* which appears later in this book, I will go over the step-by-step process for using an iPhone to film, edit, and upload videos. Many YouTube creators start with an iPhone, although some use an Android phone.

Either an iPhone, Android or a DSLR camera works best for filming YouTube videos. Many successful YouTube creators offer videos explaining their filming process along with the cameras they use. The best advice I can give you is to search YouTube for "best cameras to film YouTube videos" to see what comes up. Look for the most recent videos to provide information on the latest models. DSLR cameras range from $100 to well over $2,000.

You can purchase a brand-new camera, of course, or you can search on eBay for secondhand models for much less. You will find tutorial videos on YouTube of nearly every camera ever made, so you will be able to find help regardless of what camera you eventually end up with.

As a basic guideline, you want a camera that can film in HD, whether 720p or 1080p. HD (high definition) is the highest quality filming available for personal cameras and results in video footage that appears super crisp and clear.

Most phones even film in HD these days, including the iPhone I use. While I upload from my iPhone directly to YouTube, you will need to transfer your video footage to your computer via the camera's SD memory card if you use a stand-alone camera. Most creators who use this method rely on memory cards to hold and transfer footage and multiple batteries to keep their cameras working. And some creators still film additional footage on their phones.

The most popular DSLR cameras currently being used to make YouTube videos are:

1. **Canon PowerShot G7 X Mark III:** A compact favorite of vloggers who film in 4K with a starting price of $600.
2. **Sony ZV-1:** Another compact video camera with 4K video resolution and a starting price of $700.
3. **DJI Pocket 2:** Offers excellent stability and straightforward operation with a starting price of $350.
4. **GoPro Hero2:** Popular because of its excellent stabilization, but you may want to add an external microphone. The price starts at $400.
5. **DJI Osmo Action:** Dubbed the "best YouTube action camera for novices," this waterproof camera is super affordable at under $200.
6. **Sony A6600:** One of the most expensive vlogging cameras available at under $1400. However, the battery life and storage make it popular for taking a lot of footage.
7. **Canon EOS M6 Mark II:** High-resolution camera starting at $800.

8. **Panasonic Lumix GH5 II:** A great choice for both still shots and video, but with a hefty starting price of $2000.
9. **Sigma fp:** The smallest full-frame camera also streams over USB and has a starting price of $1700.
10. **Samsung Galaxy S21 Ultra:** This phone also shoots in 8K, making it even better than the iPhone, with a price of $900.

If you already own a DSLR camera, see if you can use it for filming before investing in a new model. Again, do a YouTube search of the model camera you own and see if you can find tutorials about how to use it for filming videos. Chances are, at least one other person is filming their YouTube videos with the same camera you already own.

HOW TO FILM ON AN SMARTPHONE:

1. **Clean the Lens:** Make sure the camera lens, both the front and back, is clean and free from smudges or dirt. The lens can fog over in heat and humidity, so be sure to keep wiping it off when filming outside.
2. **Set Up Your Shot:** Find a stable surface or use a tripod to avoid shaky footage. The set up doesn't have to be fancy; many times I simply prop my phone up on a stack of books.
3. **Turn Your Phone Horizontally:** One of the biggest mistakes new YouTubers make is holding their phone vertically, the same way they use it to facetime or use social media. Filming a video this way will create black bars on either side of the video. You need to turn the camera horizontally to avoid this.
4. **Start Recording:** Tap the red record button to begin filming and tap it again to stop. A timer will be visible to you on screen as you are filming.
5. **Save Clips:** All of your video clips will save automatically to your phone's camera roll. You will access the camera roll later when you put the clips together and edit your video. We will

cover this step later on in this book.

HOW TO FILM ON A DSRL CAMERA:

1. **Choose Your Settings:** Set your camera mode to Video or Movie and select the video resolution and frame rate. Most YouTube videos are filmed in 1080p at 30fps.
2. **Manual Mode:** Make sure the camera is on manual mode to have better control over settings.
3. **Set Up Your Shot:** Make sure your camera is set on a steady surface or a tripod for filming. If you are vlogging, a hand-held portable tripod will give you added control, although many vloggers simply hold their phones in their hands or use a GoPro.
4. **Learn the Settings:** The fancier the camera, the more settings will be available. It will be up to you to research things like aperture, shutter speed, white balance, focus, audio, stabilization, and exposure for the camera you are using. Unless you are already familiar with cameras, this is why it is best to start with a phone or basic camera.
5. **Recording:** There will be a dedicated video recording button on your camera.
6. **Save Your Clips:** Digital cameras rely on memory cards to store large amounts of video. You remove this card from your camera and insert it into your computer to transfer footage (this can also be done using a USB port that connects your camera directly to your computer).

CHAPTER FOUR: VIDEO EDITING SOFTWARE

Just as there are multiple options for cameras, there are a lot of different software programs you can use to edit your YouTube videos. I personally just use the free **iMovie app** on my iPhone to edit my YouTube videos. The iMovie app is also available for Apple laptops and computers. It is the most popular video editing software as it is easy to use and comes with most Mac computer systems.

Here are the steps to **edit YouTube videos using the iMovie app on a phone:**

1. **Select Movie:** Open the app and select **Movie** from the options on the screen.
2. **Create Movie:** The app will open your camera roll. Click on **Create Movie** at the bottom of the screen.
3. **Add Clips:** Tap the **+ sign** to add videos, phones, or audio. A new window will open. Click on **Video**. Another window will open. Select **Recently Added** to access your most recent clips. Tap each clip and click on the **+ sign** to add each to your video.
4. **Edit Clips:** Once all of your clips are added, watch the video from the beginning to see if there are sections you need to remove or shorten. Tapping on each clip will bring up options including *Split, Detach, Duplicate*, and *Delete*.
5. **Add Effects:** Tapping on each clip will also bring up additional effects you can play around with, including *Freeze, Add, Reset, Volume*, and the ability to *Add Text* and *Change Color*.
6. **Save:** Once you have finished editing, click on **Done**. Then click on the Up **Arrow** at the bottom of the screen and click

Save Video, which will save the complete video to your camera roll. From there, you can upload the video to your channel through the YouTube app.

Here are the steps to **edit YouTube videos using the iMovie app on a computer:**

1. **Import Footage:** Launch the iMovie app. Create a new project and choose a suitable aspect ratio for your YouTube video. Import your video footage by selecting **Import Media** and browsing your device for the files.
2. **Organize Clips:** Drag and drop your imported clips into the timeline in the order you want them to appear in the final video.
3. **Trim and Split Clips:** Select a clip in the timeline to reveal the editing tools. Trim the beginning and end of clips by dragging the handles. Split a clip into smaller sections using the **Split** tool.
4. **Arrange Clips:** Rearrange clips by dragging them around the timeline to create the desired sequence.
5. **Add Transitions:** Select the **Transitions** tab and browse through available transition effects. Drag and drop a transition between two clips to create a smooth visual transition.
6. **Add Music and Sound Effects:** Import music or sound effects by selecting **Import Media** again. Drag the audio file onto the timeline's audio track. Adjust the audio levels to balance the volume between your footage and the audio.
7. **Add Titles and Text:** Select the **Titles** tab and choose a title style that suits your video. Drag and drop the title onto the timeline above the desired clip. Customize the title's *Text, Font, Color,* and *Duration.*
8. **Add Effects and Filters:** Select a clip and go to the **Video**

Effects tab. Browse through available effects and filters to enhance your footage. Drag and drop the chosen effect onto the clip.

9. **Add Transitions:** Select the **Transitions** tab and browse through available transition effects. Drag and drop a transition between two clips to create a smooth visual transition.

10. **Export Your Video:** Preview your edited video to ensure everything looks and sounds as intended. Click the **File** menu and select **Share**. Choose **File** to export the video to your desired format and resolution. Follow the prompts to save the video to your computer.

11. **Upload to YouTube:** Go to the YouTube website and sign in to your account. Click the **Upload** button and select the video file you exported from iMovie. Fill in video details, such as *Title, Description, Tags*, and *Privacy* settings. Click **Publish** to make your edited video live on YouTube.

If you cannot or do not want to use iMovie, there are other options available, including:

- **Premiere Pro:** Available for both Windows and Mac, Premiere Pro is a favorite among YouTube creators. Subscriptions start at $21 a month and go up depending on features.
- **Final Cut Pro:** Available for Mac only for a one-time cost of $299.99 directly from Apple. Final Cut Pro is used by professional film editors and YouTuber creators but might be too sophisticated for newbies.
- **Premiere Elements:** Available for both Windows and Mac for a one-time cost of $99.99 from Adobe. The simple interface is suitable for beginners as it is a watered-down version of Premiere Pro.

- **Pinnacle Studio 24**: Available for Windows. Prices start at $45, depending on the store. Pinnacle Studio is an excellent option for beginners.
- **CyberLink Power Director 365**: Available for both Windows and Mac starting at $29.99 a month. It is easy to use but also offers some advanced options.
- **Premiere Rush**: Available for Android and iOS from $9.99 to $52.99 per month. If you want to use your Android device to film videos, this is the app you want to use.
- **Vimeo**: This lets you piece photos and videos together and add other elements. They offer a free version and paid plans of $55 a month.

If you are completely new to filming videos and have a smartphone, I urge you to start with that. You don't want to invest in a camera and software until you are sure you enjoy YouTube and want to build a channel.

If you do own a camera, I suggest you do the same for video editing software as I recommended for vlogging cameras: Do your research by seeing what other YouTube creators are using. A simple search of "best video editing software" on YouTube will yield many results. Many YouTube creators also put links to the items they use in the description boxes under their videos.

See if some channels you currently enjoy watching have their editing software linked. You may find that you already have an editing program installed, one that came with your computer. Again, do a YouTube search of what you already have to see if other YouTube creators are also using the same program.

As with cameras, new software options and updates are continually being released. Plus, what software you need depends on your computer system (Mac or PC) and your skill level. As always, see if you

have something already installed on your phone or computer that will
work before investing in new software.

CHAPTER FIVE: ADDITIONAL YOUTUBE EQUIPMENT

While cameras and editing software are the two most important pieces of equipment you will need to start a YouTube channel, there are other things you need to consider, including:

Computer: While I do most of my YouTube work on my iPhone, I still utilize my laptop for my videos. I find it much easier to type in my titles and description box information using my computer versus my small phone keyboard. I also like accessing the *YouTube Studio* feature from my desktop to adjust my video specifics and monetization settings. While there is a *YouTube Studio* app on my iPhone, I still prefer the full version of the website for completing specific tasks.

Fortunately, *YouTube Studio* is accessible via the internet and works with Macs and PCs. So, the computer you use for editing videos will work just fine for any other YouTube work you do as long as it has an internet connection.

While I use my Apple iPhone to film, edit, and upload my videos, I use an HP laptop with Microsoft software to access the internet and complete the backend work on my videos. Yes, I use a combination of both Apple and Microsoft products to manage my YouTube channel!

While most large YouTube channels rely on Mac computers to edit, there are options for PC users as well. The Microsoft Surface, HP, and Dell computers are used by many creators. A powerful and fast processor is the most critical factor you will want to consider in any computer you intend to use to run a YouTube channel (or, frankly, any online business). When I purchase a new computer, I buy one with the fastest processor I can afford as processing speed affects all of my computer work, not just YouTube.

If you are completely clueless about computers, simply visit a store that sells computers, such as Apple or Best Buy, and ask an associate which models have the most powerful and fastest processors. Tell them you will be using the computer to edit and upload videos. Office supply stores such as Staples and OfficeMax also have a large selection of computers and associates who can assist you. And while the employees at warehouse clubs such as Sam's Club and Costco may not have the largest selection, they often offer the best prices.

A few years back, I needed to upgrade my laptop, and I asked an associate at Sam's Club which laptop had the best processor. He showed me their two best options, and I chose from there. Now I typically only buy my computers from Sam's Club as they have the best prices. Costco also has great deals on computers. And all stores clearance their computers regularly as new models are constantly being released.

If you already use your computer for gaming, it is likely powerful enough to handle YouTube, too. The speed and power of your computer are only important if you plan to edit and upload videos on it.

Internet Connection: Having a fast, reliable internet connection is essential if you intend to use your computer to edit and upload videos. I use my iPhone because the upload speed is considerably higher than if I uploaded videos on my laptop. If you are an avid YouTube watcher, you have likely heard creators complain about the time it takes to upload their videos. So, if you still use a dial-up modem to access the World Wide Web, it is time to upgrade.

These days, most internet service providers offer various speeds of high-speed internet. I recommend going with the fastest one you can afford. I firmly believe that time is money, and I need my internet connection to work as quickly as possible for me to run all my businesses, including YouTube.

If you do not have internet access where you live and cannot obtain it, you can access the internet at your local library. Many public places now also have free WIFI. And if you are using your iPhone to film, edit, and upload videos, you only need your cell service to complete most YouTube tasks using your cell service. I have high-speed internet at home, but if it goes out, I use the hot spot feature on my iPhone to get internet access back on my computer.

LIGHTING: If you intend to film vlog-style videos, i.e., footage of you as you go about your everyday life, then you will not have to worry about purchasing lighting equipment as you will be using whatever light happens to be available in the setting you are filming in, including natural light. There are small ring lights that you can attach to your camera or phone to provide better lighting if you need it, such as if you are vlogging in the evening or inside. However, always be aware of others around you who may not want the extra light your ring light would give off.

If you plan to film exclusively inside, you can purchase several kinds of lights, everything from single-ring lights to multi-lighting systems. However, if you have a large window that lets in a lot of natural light, you may be able to get away with using just the window for lighting when filming sit-down videos inside.

However, even if you have a window with natural light, you may still want some additional lighting when filming. Many YouTube creators use studio lighting or a ring light when they film. Ring lights vary in size from tabletop to floor length. You can even purchase small ring lights that attach to your iPhone.

A search of "YouTube lights" on Amazon or other tech shopping sites will bring up a long list of options with prices from $30 and going up into the hundreds. Options range from single-light setups to complex multi-piece systems. A simple 10" ring light with a tripod stand is a great option to start with. As I suggested with cameras, search YouTube for "video lighting" to see suggestions from other creators.

Small ring lights are becoming more and more commonplace, meaning you can find portable ones for as low as $5 at Target, Walmart, and even dollar stores. However, remember that you get what you pay for. A ring light that doesn't properly attach to your camera or stand well on a tabletop is a waste of money, especially when you could have purchased a better-quality light for not a lot more money.

Remember again that it is okay to start with what you have. A window and a lamp can do wonders for your video lighting. I film my indoor at-home videos using natural light supplemented by lamps. And I don't use extra lighting when filming outside of my home, whether I am indoors or out. As your YouTube journey progresses, you can always explore more expensive options if you feel they are necessary.

Microphone: When it comes to filming YouTube videos, iPhones and most digital cameras come with built-in microphones. However, as you continue your YouTube journey, you may want to invest in additional microphones, both for sit-down videos and when you are vlogging.

Microphones come in all configurations, from desktop models to headsets, portable, noise buffering, and even clip-on. Prices vary wildly, too.

If a separate microphone will benefit you is something you will likely only discover after you have been creating videos for a while. For instance, if you film mostly vlog-style videos, you may want a microphone with a windscreen (a small bushy attachment that looks like a rabbit foot) as it will help filter out background noise such as wind.

If you find yourself drawn to creating sit-down videos and even interviews, a desktop microphone might become something you feel you need for your business. Microphones start at around $25 and can be purchased on Amazon or electronic stores such as Best Buy.

Microphones, like professional lighting and fancy cameras, are things you can add later in your YouTube career. Unless your phone or camera cannot record sound, there is no need to invest in one right away.

Tripod: Tripods are another item you might be able to delay buying or skip altogether. If you plan only to vlog, your hand will serve as your tripod. However, I do have a hand-help grip that I use on my phone when vlogging. It also works as a stand as it holds my phone upright when I am filming a sit-down video.

I went for years without a tripod but finally spent $70 on a good model with a solid base and a ring light attached. However, for years I just propped my phone up on books and boxes to film!

I have seen YouTube creators prop their cameras and phones up in various ways: on stacks of books, nestled into cabinets, or even on open shelves. If you buy a lighting kit, even a basic ring light, it will often come with a tripod to which you can attach a camera or phone. There are even portable tripods that come with a small ring light attached for use when you are on the go.

The benefits of a tripod are that it keeps your filming device steady and set at the angle you choose. It can be a little more work to get the right angle when you simply set your camera onto a flat surface or what you think is a flat surface. I still run into issues keeping my camera steady on a table even when using my new stand, as the table itself is unsteady. Even with a new device, I sometimes still just prop my phone up to film.

See how you get by without using a tripod before buying one. There are all styles and sizes available on sites like Amazon that start at around $15. However, I recommend investing in something with a weighted bottom to keep the camera steady.

PRO TIP: You will hear many YouTube creators tout the benefits of expensive filming equipment. Note that most of these recommendations also include affiliate links where the person is earning money for every item they sell. This doesn't mean the equipment isn't worth it, but it just may not be worth it for you at the moment. Don't let yourself get caught up in FOMO, i.e. "fear of missing out" when it comes to buying equipment for your YouTube channel!

CHAPTER SIX: YOUTUBE FILMING TIPS

So, you have figured out which camera and editing software you need to start your YouTube channel along with things such as a computer and internet access. That covers the equipment side of things.

But there are other things to consider when you are filming YouTube videos that do not cost you any money but are just as important as those. And these are things that you will only learn through trial and error. Your first few attempts at filming likely won't be your best, but they will be a valuable learning experience for you.

Light: Lighting is the biggest issue for most YouTube creators, me included. As I discussed earlier, natural light (either outside or through a window) can provide you with excellent lighting, although you may decide to upgrade to professional lights. Ring lights come in all sizes, from small portable versions attached to your iPhone to full-size models that take up half a room.

I rely on natural light when vlogging outdoors, and stores are often well-lit enough for me if I am vlogging while shopping. At home, I rely on a large window and a lamp. Whether you decide to invest in lighting or make do with what you have on hand, making sure your videos are well-lit is essential to your channel growth. Having light in front of you, rather than behind, will illuminate your face versus creating a shadow.

Most cameras and phones come with flash settings that can help illuminate your settings and cause things to look unnatural. Eyes, for one thing, can appear red when a flash is used. Always make sure to rewatch your footage and refilm if necessary.

Steady Hand: Nothing is worse than watching shaky camera footage, and I have been guilty of doing this myself while vlogging. As we discussed in the previous chapter, a tripod can come in handy. A hand-held stand or tripod can help tremendously with making sure your videos aren't jumpy.

If you are filming a sit-down video with the camera in one place, make sure it is on a flat, steady surface and that it is not moving around while you are filming. Placing your computer at eye level is important, even if that means you prop your camera up on a stack of books. Ensure the set up isn't wobbly.

I also run into issues of accidentally getting my fingers in the shot while filming with my iPhone. Sometimes I realize I want to vlog something but forgot my hand-help tripod. I end up placing my finger too close to the lens, and images of my blurry finger appear in the picture. I can't tell you how many times I've had to delete otherwise good footage because of my blurry finger!

Your Voice: A big problem I see with many new YouTube creators is their low video volume; I cannot even hear what they are saying. When filming, make sure you speak in a clear, loud voice. While you do not want to scream at your viewers, you want to make sure they can hear what you are saying. Practice speaking at different volumes to find what sounds best when played back.

Talking too fast or too slow can also turn off viewers. I struggle with speaking too quickly and must continually remind myself to slow my speech and speak reasonably, making sure to enunciate my words so that viewers can understand what I am saying. You can also add captions to your videos.

Making sure you speak clearly is also essential when filming videos. As I mentioned, in my everyday life, I tend to talk fast and fill my speech with slang. But to appeal to a worldwide audience, I make sure to speak slowly and clearly and avoid saying "like" and "um" throughout my videos. And if possible, avoid complicated vocabulary as you want to attract viewers of all ages, abilities, and locations.

Background Noise: Ensure there is no background noise while filming, such as music or the television. Not only will background noise interfere with viewers hearing what you are saying, but often background noise is copyrighted, which means it may prevent you from monetizing your videos. If you are filming in public, there will likely be background noise. Make sure you hold your camera close when speaking to ensure your viewers hear you over the noise.

You can also do voiceovers for videos filmed in very loud locations. If you are filming in a store where the music is very loud, you can film your footage but then do a voiceover during the editing process. You can do a voiceover easily using the iMovie app on both a phone and desktop computer.

If filming at home, turn your phone to silent and film in a quiet room with a closed door. If you live with other people, let them know when you are filming and ask them to keep noise and interruptions to a minimum. If you have a dog that barks or pets that will distract you, it may be best to place them elsewhere in your home while filming. Or you may find that you need to leave your house to film, hence why many vloggers film in their cars!

I have dogs, so trust me when I say they can be as distracting as young children when I try to film. I schedule my at-home filming during times when they are napping. Stay-at-home parents may reserve their filming for when their children are in school. Removing distractions also means your filming process will go much faster, so you can get back to your family and pets sooner. The more you have to stop and start filming, the longer it will take to complete a video.

If you are vlogging, ensure your hand does not inadvertently cover up the microphone. Also, please be aware that most music is copyrighted, meaning you will not be able to monetize videos where background music is being played, such as in stores or tourist attractions. As I mentioned, you may need to do voiceover commentary or overlay the footage with music that has a free license.

Copyright Music: The most challenging part of vlogging is ensuring the microphone picks up no copyrighted music. Nothing is worse than taking the time to vlog only to have YouTube put a copyright strike on the video due to music in the background. While the video will usually still be eligible to be viewed, it will be ineligible to earn you any AdSense.

I've had entire Disney vlogs demonetized due to the music. One trick you can use is to have YouTube narrow down where copyrighted music is in your video and allow them to trim it out. This process can take a day or two, but it can save a video you've already finished versus refilming it.

You can also mute the sound when you are vlogging in public and do a voiceover later. This, of course, takes more work. I try to avoid the music altogether.

Personal: I edit out sneezes and coughs. Having some water nearby is helpful to stay hydrated while filming so that your speech remains as clear as possible. Lip balm is also handy to keep your lips from drying out, which can negatively affect your speech. A little makeup can also go a long way towards looking your best. A little powder to control shine can make a huge difference.

Be careful about giving out too much personal information in your videos. Don't show the front of your house, make sure papers with personal information aren't shown on camera, and don't broadcast where you are traveling until you are back home. The last thing you want when you are on vacation is for viewers to follow you. And it's never a good idea to announce when your house is empty as that information can lead to a break-in.

Try not to film other people in your vlogs, such as other customers, inside a store. While it is normal to catch a glimpse of a stranger's back in a vlog, you do not want a video filmed with a stranger's face looking right into the camera. Many people vlog with the camera lens focused on them, while others may film with someone else, and the person with the camera focuses on the second person. I vlog a lot in public, and it's often nearly impossible not to have glimpses of other people in the shots, but I do the best I can do avoid it.

If you smoke, do not smoke on camera. Avoid chewing gum while filming. Be aware of your language; swearing not only turns off viewers but it can result in YouTube demonetizing your videos. And do your best to clean up your surrounding area. No one wants to see your overflowing trash can or a pile of dirty laundry in the background of your videos.

Quality: No matter what equipment you use to film, edit, and upload your YouTube videos, producing high-quality videos is vital. As I have said several times, you don't need to invest in fancy equipment, at least not initially, so you must do the very best you can with what you have. You don't need the most expensive camera to make quality videos or expensive editing software.

Even though I film on my iPhone, I still upload my videos in High Definition. iPhones let you film in 720p, 1080p, and 4K. Choose 4K if possible, although both 720p and 1080p are still excellent. The difference will come in the upload speed. I often do not have the time to allow my videos to upload in 1080p or 4K as I need my iPhone for other work. But I film, edit, and upload videos completely from my iPhone using the iMovie and YouTube apps, both of which are free to download.

But if you have the option, always choose the highest resolution possible. YouTube and viewers both favor videos shot in the highest definition possible. If I have a particularly long video, I will turn the screensaver off, plug my phone into a charger, and start the upload process to run overnight. Depending on the speed of your Wifi connection, it can take minutes or hours to upload videos.

Backgrounds: You have likely seen YouTube videos with professionally designed backgrounds and those shot in what looks like a hoarder's home. While you do not need to spend thousands of dollars to make the background of your videos look like it came straight from a home decor magazine, you want to make sure to film in a clean, clutter-free space with a simple backdrop.

I have a dedicated space in my office where I film sit-down videos. I have bookshelves behind me, and I change the décor on the shelves seasonally. In the past, I will admit that my backgrounds were not as nice as I would have liked them to be, especially ones where there were piles of eBay inventory behind me (although, in my defense, I was filming videos about eBay!).

You want your background to complement the subject of your videos. My eBay videos were a bit cluttered, but, again, eBay was my full-time job, and other eBay sellers, who understood about having a lot of stuff, were the ones who watched my videos. So, it wasn't as big of an issue. But if you are filming cooking videos, you don't want viewers to see a dirty kitchen. If you are filming a tutorial about a specific product, you don't want a bunch of non-related items clogging up the screen.

I am always trying to improve the quality of my videos, including my backgrounds. Note that if you are vlogging, you do not have to worry about creating a pretty backdrop as you will be filming yourself in whatever place you happen to be. However, you still want to be aware of your surroundings so that viewers focus on you, not on what might be happening in the shot behind you.

One of my favorite backgrounds that I see many female YouTubers use is to film with their bed behind them, and twinkle lights (the kind you put on Christmas trees) strung up around the bed frame or window. This lighting arrangement creates such a lovely scene for filming. Shelves with minimal decorations also create a nice backdrop.

Other people film with the nicest part of their kitchen or living room behind them. Gamers and review channels often have bookshelves behind them full of neatly arranged products. Beauty channels often have some makeup products in the background. You want your background to align with your content. For instance, if you film cooking videos, you will want to use your kitchen as your backdrop, not your dirty garage.

When in doubt, a plain wall always makes a great backdrop, especially if it is next to a window that provides natural light. If you are filming in a room with sparse decorations and furniture, test your audio to make sure there is no echo when speaking. Adding a rug on top of a hardwood floor can help buffer an echo in an empty room.

Watch YouTube videos from creators in the same category you are in to see their backgrounds. While you never want to copy someone else, if you see that most YouTubers in your category are filming with a plain background, you should follow their lead. Conversely, if they are filming with a lot of decorations in their background, you may want to do that, too.

Dedicated Space: If you are serious about making sit-down YouTube videos that you can grow into a business that earns you a decent income, you will want to consider dedicating a space for filming that is well-lit and nicely decorated. A set up next to a window with a clean background, a nice chair, and a steady table are all you need to create a professional setting.

However, if you are just starting out or are only interested in making a bit of money from YouTube, do your best with what you have. Some of the biggest YouTube channels on the site today got their start with the creators filming while sitting on the floor of their bedrooms or even sitting in their cars with the cameras propped up on their steering wheels. I've seen full-time YouTube creators film their videos with their cameras stacked atop empty shoe boxes. Or they film exclusively from their cars!

Camera Angle: Finding the angle from which you look your best on camera can be challenging. Most of us feel we have a "good side," the side of our face from which we look a bit more attractive than the other. However, video is much different from still photography in that you move around on film and are not sitting in a stationary position. Therefore, it is more important to have the camera facing you directly and slightly above you. Having to look up a bit at the camera helps eliminate the double chin phenomenon!

As with the background, the camera angle is something I have constantly been challenged by. I've tried numerous tripods over the years for my iPhone, but most were flimsy. I finally invested in a $70 model with a strong base that holds my phone steady and has an attached ring light. However, I still sometimes find myself propping my phone up on a stack of books to film!

When vlogging, I now have a portable hand-held tripod that I can attach to my phone that also converts to a stand; I can just prop the stand up on a flat surface to film when I am on the go. And the handle helps me hold the camera steady when I am vlogging. A stick-on holder such as a pop-socket type device that gives your fingers something to firmly grasp also helps.

Of course, if you choose not to appear on screen, you don't focus on how you look but on what you are filming, whether it is a single stationary item or a moving scene. For instance, if you are filming cooking videos, you will want a tripod holding the camera to look over what you are preparing. If you are filming review videos, you want your camera trained on the item you are reviewing.

Or perhaps you can have someone else hold the camera and film you. You will notice that many vloggers film in pairs so that one is always holding the camera while the other is in front of it.

Grooming: If you are doing close-up shots of your hands, make sure your nails are trim and clean. Nothing turns viewers off more than dirty fingernails and bloody cuticles. If you are filming your hands a lot, a professional manicure is a good investment, and it is also a tax write-off as it is a business expense!

Make sure your clothes are clean and tidy. While you don't need to wear designer clothing, make sure what you do have on isn't stained or torn. Also, avoid busy patterns as they don't appear well on camera.

While you do not have to have your hair and make-up professionally done every time you film a YouTube video, you do want to take care of your appearance. Looking as clean and neat as possible goes a long way toward presenting yourself in the best possible light, even if you are simply wearing jeans and a plain tee shirt. A bit of powder on both men and women can help eliminate shine. A bit of lip balm makes your lips look smooth. Even a touch of mascara can help your eyes pop on camera.

As I mentioned earlier, clean nails, and hands overall, are so important, if you are filming close-up shots with your hands. Try to prepare yourself as you would if you were going on a job interview or first date when your clothing and appearance are at your best. You don't have to have a full face of makeup or have your hair professionally styled, but a clean face and freshly brushed hair are a must. Remember that you are trying to appeal to a broad audience of viewers and present yourself accordingly.

Preview Before Uploading: I have watched some horrible YouTube videos over the years, ones where the footage is dark, the volume is on mute, and the screen is jerky. I have even seen videos that were upside down! Before you make your videos live, preview them first. While they do not have to be up to the Hollywood standard of film quality, you want them to be as clear and steady as possible. If a video looks terrible to you while previewing it, imagine what viewers will think when you upload it.

Redo videos that are not of good quality. Practice makes perfect! I have re-filmed many videos during my time on YouTube. I know that having to re-film a video is frustrating. Still, I would rather take the time to completely redo a video than have a poor-quality clip be viewed by thousands and potentially millions of people. One poorly filmed video could cost me new subscribers and worse, lose the ones I already have. Therefore, I would rather have no video than a poorly filmed one.

Please don't be upset if your first videos don't look that great, as it takes time to learn your best filming style. Try different angles and methods until you find what you are most comfortable with. I have put many of my older videos on "private," as the quality is terrible! Presenting yourself in the best possible light is more valuable than any expensive camera.

CHAPTER SEVEN: CHOOSING A CHANNEL THEME

As I talked about in the *Introduction* of this book, my first YouTube channel was dedicated solely to my eBay reselling business. My videos showed viewers the items I sourced at estate sales and thrift stores to sell online, along with all my tips and tricks for making money on eBay. I did not really talk about anything else but reselling on that channel, and the people who subscribed to me were there to learn and/or talk about eBay, too.

I also talked about how when I started my first YouTube channel I signed up under a non-Google email (which, I remind you, you can no longer do; so, no worries that you will make the same mistake that I did) and that I was not able to monetize my first channel. It took starting a second channel under a Google account that allowed me to earn AdSense income from my videos.

When I first started YouTube, I was unaware that you could make money on the site. I was happy to just connect with other resellers and share what I knew. It was a small community, and it really helped me change the direction of my online selling business. If you will remember from the *Introduction*, I was struggling to figure out a new direction for my business; the videos I found on YouTube helped me do just that.

However, I will also be honest and tell you that once I realized the possibility of making money on YouTube, I made the leap and started a new channel. I deleted the first channel and focused on my newly created one because I still enjoyed being on the site and wanted to earn money from my videos. By that time, I had started a money-saving blog and named my new channel after that. However, my content is still heavily focused on eBay. I then started another channel dedicated to Walt Disney World vacation vlogs.

That changed over the years, as I have already discussed. From reselling content to couponing and traveling to cooking, my content across my channels has been all over the place. And that has caused my channels to struggle. The constant change in content and my posting schedule threw my YouTube algorithm for a loop, and YouTube punished me by suppressing my channels and placing low-dollar ads on my videos. Hence I now focus on one main channel where I film vlog-style videos three times a week.

However, you do not have to make the same mistakes I have. I have learned the hard way what works and what does not, and this book is my way of passing that information on to you. Not that you won't make mistakes along the way. We all do. But I hope you can look at those mistakes as learning lessons. Fortunately, if you are just starting your YouTube journey, millions of other creators have paved the way for you, whose lessons you can learn from.

So, what is the biggest lesson I can share with you?

Figure out your channel's theme and stick to it!

Mixing business content with lifestyle content did not work for me, and my AdSense earnings dropped because of it. You need to figure out exactly what your channel is about in order to grow your audience and income. And if you want to create drastically different content than you started with, you can do that on a second or even third channel.

Now, that does not mean you cannot film different types of videos on one channel. It just means you need to stick to one main TOPIC for your channel. For instance, I have many friends who are resellers who produce lots of different types of videos, such as "shop with me" vlogs where they go sourcing, sit-down haul videos where they share what they purchased to resell, and even live sales where viewers buy directly from them in real-time.

But while the *styles* of videos may differ, the *topic* is always the same: reselling. Those who share lifestyle videos do so on a second channel. You have likely also seen this from some of the YouTube creators you follow. Many have a channel for vlogs and a channel for sit-down videos. Some focus on one topic on one channel, such as gaming or makeup tutorials, and something absolutely different on another channel, such as travel vlogs or parenting advice. You can cover different topics on YouTube as long as you cover each on different channels.

To choose your video's category, log into your YouTube account, click on your profile icon, and then click on **YouTube Studio**. Click on **Content** to bring up your list of videos.

If you want each of your videos to be placed in different categories, you'll need to do each one individually. Click on the box on the left side next to the video and then click on **Edit** at the top of the page. Select **Category** from the drop-down menu. A new drop-down menu will appear with the **15 YouTube categories**, which we discuss further in the following section.

If you want to put all of your videos in the same category, simply select all of your videos and then click on **Edit** at the top of the page. Select **Category** from the drop-down menu and select the category to which you want your videos added.

Whether you edit each video individually or do a bulk edit, you will click on **UPDATE VIDEOS** to finish to process.

The 15 YouTube Categories: You can choose a category for your channel and individual videos. The categories are in no particular order.

1. **Film & Animation:** Movie trailers, full movies, movie scenes, songs, behind-the-scenes videos, and anything related

to films
2. **Autos & Vehicles:** Vehicle reviews, advertising, and vlogging
3. **Music:** Music videos and concert vlogs
4. **Pets & Animals:** Pet and animal education as well as pet vlogging
5. **Sports:** Athlete interviews, sporting events, and collecting
6. **Travel & Events:** Vacation vlogs, festivals, and travel advice
7. **Gaming:** Video games
8. **People & Blogs:** Everything from parenting and beauty to health and fitness
9. **Comedy:** Spoofs and pranks
10. **Entertainment:** Television, celebrities, and gossip
11. **News & Politics:** Current events
12. **How-to & Style:** Tutorials, fashion, organization, and home
13. **Education:** Home-schooling, teaching, lectures, and history
14. **Science & Technology:** Space, new inventions, and educational content
15. **Nonprofits & Activism:** Social causes

Starting out, I would recommend you begin with just ONE YouTube channel and commit to focusing on one category. You want to master running a single channel and learning one category before thinking about having two...or more. Yes, some people have three or even four channels. However, most YouTube creators only have one channel, so do not panic if you can only see yourself with one, as it is totally normal.

You may start your channel creating one type of content but quickly realize it's not for you. It's okay to change course in the beginning before you have built up an audience. You just don't want to change from filming prank videos to creating gardening videos after you've built up your channel on the former over several years.

But if the videos you intend to share all fall under the same general theme, such as lifestyle or gaming, then you will be just fine with all your content on one channel. And it's not like you can't mix some other content within the same video. Maybe you normally film makeup tutorials but take a yearly vacation to Walt Disney World. You could easily add a vacation vlog to your schedule without completely throwing off your algorithm. And you never know sometimes, what you think your viewers won't be interested in ends up being more popular than what you've been uploading!

When I first started on YouTube, I viewed having a channel like having your own television network. I thought that my channel was like a network in my cable lineup. I believed that I could have different types of "shows" on my channel and that viewers would just pick the videos they wanted to watch.

Unfortunately, that is not the way viewers behave on YouTube. While you have NBC in your television channel line-up, it is likely that you only watch a few of the shows on the NBC network. However, you do not take NBC out of your television package just because you do not watch every show they air. You watch the shows you want to and simply ignore the rest.

YouTube, however, is different. Viewers look at the entire YouTube site as a whole as if it were a television network, with the individual channels functioning as separate shows. They view YouTube like NBC; they have the YouTube app installed on their phone the way we have NBC automatically in our television line-up. And just like NBC has different types of television shows, YouTube has different types of channels.

You have YouTube on your smartphone or computer and watch the "shows," i.e., the channels you like. However, you do not watch ALL the channels because you are not interested in all the different "shows." But you keep YouTube installed on your devices the same way you keep the various networks, such as NBC, installed on your television lineup.

Think of it like this: Say your favorite television show is *Law & Order: SVU*, which still airs on the NBC television network, but it is now also shown on many other channels and even streaming services via syndication. Imagine if you are happily watching an episode of *SVU*, but then the following show to air was *America's Got Talent*, another NBC staple. Now, you may like *AGT*, but for this example, let's say that you do not. If you were watching *SVU* on your television or streaming service and *AGT* suddenly came on, you would just change the channel to a different show, right?

However, what if *SVU* had its very own dedicated television channel? You would need to subscribe to this channel separately from your other television channels. But since *SVU* is your absolute favorite show, you are thrilled to be able to subscribe to a channel that is dedicated only to *SVU*.

But imagine one day when you went to watch *SVU* on this dedicated channel, they suddenly started showing *AGT* episodes.

Suddenly this unique channel that you only subscribed to so that you could watch *SVU* is showing you a completely different show, making it hard for you even to find the episodes of *SVU* that you want to watch.

Would you stay subscribed to the channel or look for better content elsewhere? If this select *SVU* channel were a YouTube channel, most YouTube subscribers would unsubscribe once other shows were introduced. They would then find a different channel focused only on *SVU*, leaving the first channel to die out.

Some YouTube viewers will subscribe and stay subscribed to channels because they like all or at least most of the "shows" (individual videos) that are being uploaded. However, suppose they start to dislike more "shows" (individual videos) than they actually like. In that case, they may unsubscribe from that channel and search out different channels to subscribe to, ones that provide them with the content they want.

You want to keep your audience and not drive them away, which is why it is so important to stick to the theme of your channel! If you have a beauty channel, stick to beauty-related content. If you have a travel channel, stick to travel-related content.

Trying to mix vacation vlogs with reselling videos was a disaster for me as it confused my viewers as to what my channel (i.e., the "shows") was about, and I lost subscribers because of it. And when I tried to rebrand my channels completely (I dabbled in everything from product reviews, subscription boxes, shopping hauls, and even a reselling podcast), I further lost viewers. And when subscribers dropped off, YouTube stopped showing my videos to potential new viewers.

I had to regroup and start fresh, committing to ONE type of content on ONE channel and sticking to that, even if that meant I was starting from scratch to rebuild my viewership. Just because my main channel has nearly 30,000 subscribers doesn't mean my videos get 30,000 views. When I was changing my content, I was lucky to get 1,000 views on a video. It was a scary time, and it almost made me quit YouTube.

These days I have my main channel, *Ann Eckhart*, where I upload all videos, most of which are vlogs. Some viewers love vlogs; some viewers hate them. Some viewers love sit-down videos; other viewers hate them. I had to do what was best for me, however, and vlogging is what works for me.

However, at the end of the day, no matter what I am vlogging about or how much engagement I am getting, I try only to make videos that I WANT to make, ones that are FUN and INTERESTING to me. Even though I am now earning money on YouTube, I mainly make videos for my own personal enjoyment.

YouTube has improved my public speaking skills and increased my confidence. It has allowed me to network and make new friends with people I would have never met otherwise. It has also helped me grow my book sales, make money from sponsorships, get free products, and in 2022, launch an Etsy shop. I make YouTube videos for FUN, and as a bonus, I also earn a PROFIT. Plus they are a form of advertising for all of my businesses, which earns me more money.

While I have covered a wide variety of topics in my years on YouTube, you are likely looking to only film videos on one subject. Do not follow the trends to go with what is popular. Make videos about what you LOVE, and the subscribers, and AdSense revenue, will follow.

Beauty, pranks, and gaming are huge categories on YouTube. But if you have no interest in them, why would you want to make videos on those topics? You may think that whatever it is you are interested in won't have an audience, but you are interested in it means there are other like-minded people just waiting for your content.

Every YouTube category has numerous themes that fall under it. Figuring out your channel's category is relatively easy; it's choosing the theme of your actual videos that can be tricky. Think about how viewers would describe your videos. Most viewers will think about your content in terms of theme, not necessarily categories.

Some common YouTube channel themes and video topics are as follows.

Beauty: Beauty bloggers and vloggers are all over YouTube, and they are some of the most successful channels on the site. Some YouTube "beauty gurus" have an accompanying blog to support their videos and to earn more ad revenue from their websites, but that seems to be a less popular option than it once was. Instead, YouTube creators are now using Instagram and TikTok to promote their channels.

Regardless, if you love make-up and skincare, sharing your personal tips and tricks with others may be the perfect theme for your channel. And the opportunities for content are endless, as is the possibility of brands sending you free makeup products to test on camera. Beauty channels receive the largest number of free product offers as makeup brands love the chance to have their products featured on YouTube.

In addition to doing make-up tutorials, beauty gurus also do first impression reviews of products, shopping hauls (from stores such as ULTA, Sephora, and Bath & Body Works), make-up storage, and make-up collections. Nail art also falls under the beauty umbrella, and there are entire channels devoted to nail polish storage and application.

The beauty category is very crowded on YouTube. Only start a beauty channel because you LOVE cosmetics, as the chances of success are much lower than other themes. However, if you are good at applying makeup and have a style that impresses others, the subscribers and ad revenue will follow.

Budgeting: With gas and grocery prices on the rise, many people are pinching pennies to make ends meet. Couponing, prepping, bargain shopping, and budget-friendly travel are all very popular videos on YouTube. Also popular are people documenting their journey to get out of debt.

Business: A lot of my YouTube videos over the years have fallen under the "Business" category. In addition to reselling, I am also an author and have shared videos about how I make money self-publishing. Other business topics I have made videos about include affiliate marketing, print-on-demand, and now how to run an Etsy sticker shop.

If you are in a career that others are interested in, consider sharing about it on YouTube. You may even find yourself developing courses and paid Patreon groups based on your knowledge that you can also monetize.

For instance, some of my fellow resellers have private groups that share where to source clothing from and which brands to buy. Viewers must pay for this special access, giving the channel creators an additional income stream. Other friends have created courses and have Patreon groups and merchandise, all of which earn them extra income.

Comedy & Pranks: Pranking has become a hot trend on YouTube, and some creators are making big money by putting on elaborate, often dangerous, and expensive stunts. And while this type of content is not easy to replicate, it can be done on a small scale through sketch comedy or single joke-telling. Videos like these have been an avenue for comedians looking to break into the comedy business.

Note that punk videos are geared toward children and families, and other punk videos are geared toward adults. Your channel should only focus on one of these demographics.

Cooking & Baking: Do you love to cook up new recipes or share your favorite baking creations with friends? If you enjoy being in the kitchen, you can share your culinary knowledge via YouTube videos. You do not have to be an expert chef, either; even the most straightforward recipes are popular on YouTube. In fact, sometimes simple is best as people are looking for quick and easy meal ideas.

I have posted several cooking and baking videos on my channels over the years; all my recipes are super easy to make, and I always get a lot of great feedback from viewers. Most of these videos are relatively short in length, but they are some of my top-earning AdSense videos!

If you start a cooking channel, you'll also want to create an Amazon Affiliate account so that you can link the kitchen tools you use in your videos. These links can generate additional income when people click through to Amazon and make a purchase.

Crafting: There is a vast crafting community on YouTube, so if you are a crafter, you will find others who share your passion. Whether you want to film tutorials or simply show off your craft supply hauls and projects, you will find an eager audience awaiting your content.

Beading, scrapbooking, knitting, quilting, card making, and any other type of crafting and DIY category can make for great videos, whether they are tutorials or hauls. Hauls from Hobby Lobby, Michael's, JoAnn, and even Dollar Tree can bring in a lot of views.

The crafting community on YouTube is huge, so be sure to connect with other crafters who are making videos by liking and commenting on their videos, too. I am not a crafter myself, but I have done well with some DIY Dollar Tree tutorials.

Fashion: Do you love to put together outfits? Do you like to style clothing you find at thrift stores? Do you enjoy reviewing new fashion brands? Then a fashion-themed channel may be an excellent fit for you! Figure out your niche and expand on that. Maybe you have an eye for vintage or like to create looks based on designer duds. Or maybe you enjoy styling the different body types of your friends and family. Whatever your personal style or mantra is, there is an audience for it on YouTube.

Fashion influencers also share tips on closet organization, their jewelry collections, and try-on hauls from trending online brands. Body positivity and plus-size fashion are popular online trends as people want to embrace their bodies and learn what works best on their frames.

Signing up with Amazon and other affiliates will also allow you to link your looks and make money from referrals. You've likely seen "shop my look" links on social media posts of people showing off their outfits. These links are affiliate links, meaning the creator makes money when someone clicks through to the retailer and makes a purchase.

Gaming: Video game channels are among the most popular on YouTube, with the top creators earning millions of dollars a year just by live-streaming themselves playing games. If you love to play video games, you can turn your hobby into income on YouTube.

Naturally, this will take a higher level of technology than simply filming on an iPhone, as you will be screen-sharing your video game next to a shot of you playing. But if you are already into playing video games, you likely already know how to stream that content on your computer and share it on YouTube.

Gardening: If you have a green thumb, consider sharing your gardening skills on YouTube. Many people want to learn about plants, flowers, and vegetable gardening. Prepping and off-grid living are becoming very popular topics on YouTube, and gardening fits in with those genres.

Share all your gardening information and watch your subscriber list (and AdSense money) grow along with your plants. Plus, with an Amazon Associates account, you can link the products you use and earn additional income.

Hauls & Subscription Boxes: Love to shop? Share your shopping hauls with your YouTube subscribers. Even a trip to the grocery store to stock the fridge can make for an exciting video. Trader Joe's and Costco hauls are wildly popular.

I film quite a few haul videos on my personal YouTube channel from stores such as Dollar Tree, Bath & Body Works, and Target, and they are always a big hit. Sometimes I even film "shop with me" videos and take my viewers along with me in vlog-style videos. Even grocery store hauls can bring in a large number of views.

Subscription boxes fall under the "Hauls" category, and this is something I cover extensively on my main YouTube channel. Subscription box companies offer themed boxes filled with everything from beauty products to home décor. Subscribers can get these boxes monthly or quarterly, depending on the service. Opening these boxes has become extremely popular on YouTube.

Health & Fitness: Another hot YouTube channel theme is health, specifically diet and fitness. Whether it is nutrition, weight loss, bodybuilding, or running, many people turn to YouTube to get in shape.

Natural food and specialty diets (gluten-free, vegan, raw) are also popular video topics. Even grocery hauls of healthy food from stores such as ALDI and Trader Joe's bring in viewers.

How-To & Education: As I talked about in the filming equipment section, there are thousands of how-to videos on YouTube that cover nearly every topic you can think of, including how to film and edit YouTube videos. If there is an area or area you are proficient in (computers, carpentry, crafting), creating how-to videos can be a great source of videos for your channel. Some channels are entirely dedicated to showing how to put together items purchased online.

I have recently relied on YouTube videos to show me how to build a shelf and to assemble a pressure washer, both of which I ordered on Amazon. Creators of these videos not only make money via AdSense but also from the affiliate links they provide. For instance, in the video I watched on the pressure washer, the creator linked the pressure washer in the video's description box. The creator then earned an Amazon commission from anyone who clicked on the link and made a purchase on the site.

A bonus of reviewing products is that you will be contacted by many Amazon sellers who offer you a free product in exchange for making a YouTube video about it. I have received free mattresses, pillows, vacuums, and small kitchen appliances from brands that simply want me to show their product in a video and give viewers the link to their websites.

Lifehacks: If you like to scroll through social media, chances are you stumbled upon "lifehack" posts where people share shortcuts and tricks to do everything from peeling vegetables to packing a suitcase. The possibilities of how to present this content are endless.

You can film one hack per video or put together lists such as "Top 10 Ways to Save Money Eating Out." A search of "lists" on YouTube will bring up countless options. From "Top 10 List of Disney World Rides" to the "List of Top 15 Movies of All Time," there is a list for everything. It may not seem like riveting content, but a large audience is searching for it on YouTube.

Mommy Videos: Are you a mom-to-be, or do you already have little ones in the home? There are many other mothers out there who you can connect with, whether by merely sharing your baby's milestones or talking about what you feed your toddler. Many women (and even men!) want to interact with other parents online.

Homeschooling videos are also popular, as are baby and children's product reviews. Other videos that typically receive many views are kids' clothing hauls, back-to-school hauls, child-rearing tips, and what presents parents are buying their kids for the holidays.

Organization: Organizing is another hot YouTube channel theme. How to organize your house, office, car, kid's toys, crafts, garage, and basement can all make for great videos. If you excel at organizing, you may think there is no audience for this topic, but believe me, there are people out there who would love to watch you organize something as simple as a junk drawer! Organizing your home on a budget from dollar stores is something many people produce videos on, too.

And since Amazon is full of organizing products, an Amazon Associates account will allow you to link products your viewers can shop for. Some creators only do videos with products purchased on Amazon to earn money from the affiliate links!

Restaurant & Food Reviews: If you are a foodie who loves to taste test the new dining and snack options in your area and when you travel, a channel dedicated to food reviews may be right up your alley. Whether you vlog while dining out, order fast food that you eat in your car, or do dedicated taste-testing videos at home, viewers gobble up food content.

Also under the food review category are "mukbang" videos where the creator consumes a huge quantity of food from the same restaurant while chatting on camera. Some of these are done as live streams, too.

Reviews: Do you love to read or go to the movies? Are friends always asking you to recommend your favorite video games or CDs? Do you always buy the latest gadgets? Millions of people turn to YouTube for reviews, so if you love books, movies, television, video games, music, and/or electronics, consider making a channel where you offer your opinions!

If you review products, you will soon start to be contacted by companies offering to send you free items in exchange for video reviews. In recent years I have been sent a robotic vacuum, an air fryer, a humidifier, and numerous subscription boxes, all for free, just for showing them on my YouTube channel.

If you plan to do reviews, note that copyright issues will prevent you from using clips of movies, video games, television shows, or music. Still, you can hold up your own copy of a DVD or CD if you want some type of visual; or you can add still photos from the productions.

As I've noted several times, another way to make money on your channel, including for reviews, is to sign up for an Amazon Associates account and put your referral link in the description bar to the item you are reviewing. If someone buys something through your link, whether it is the item you reviewed or something else, you will earn a commission on their purchase.

Tags: Tags are trendy amongst YouTubers. are tags galore on YouTube, giving you an easy way to create content, as all you must do is answer the questions. Tags are especially helpful if you are just starting on YouTube and unsure of what kinds of videos you want to make.

For a complete list of tags, check out the BONUS section at the end of this book where I share dozens of popular tags with you!

Thrifting: Are you a bargain hunter who loves to score the racks at Goodwill for the best deals? Do you spend your Saturday mornings driving around town in search of garage sales? If you love to thrift, an audience is waiting for you on YouTube! From shop-with-me vlogs to hauls and even DIY refurbishment of secondhand furniture, thrifting is a hot topic with an eager audience on YouTube.

As someone who thrifts to sell on eBay, there is also a large reselling community on YouTube. Creators all of ages and from all over America film videos of their hauls to sell on sites like eBay and Poshmark, along with sharing tips about the reselling business.

Travel: Do you love to travel? Perhaps you take frequent road trips or cruises, or maybe you are an RV or camping enthusiast. Many YouTube viewers would love to see your travel footage, including your packing tips, dining recommendations, and money-saving advice.

I have filmed many Walt Disney Vacation vlogs for my YouTube channel over the years, and they are always a big hit. Cruise vlogs are also extremely popular on YouTube. But even day trips around your area bring in viewers.

Vlogging: People worldwide chronicle their lives through vlogs, many doing so daily. Note that vlogging is very time-consuming and can feel like an invasion of privacy if you are not careful; however, many folks are earning a part-time and even a full-time income on YouTube by sharing 10-to-20-minute snippets of their daily lives. Note that you do not have to be a daily vlogger to have a vlog channel; you can film as many or as few vlogs as you would like, although it helps stick to a schedule, such as posting vlogs three times a week.

Suppose you enjoy vlogging but do not want to commit to a set vlogging schedule. In that case, you can simply vlog whenever you are doing something particularly exciting or during a "vlogging month" such as "Vlogmas" (vlogging for Christmas), "Vlogtober" (vlogging every day in October), "VEDA" (vlogging every day in April), or "Vlogust" (vlogging every day in August). I, myself, have done "Vlogust," "Vlogtober," and "Vlogmas" in the past.

The hard part about vlogging for me has been that the subscribers who love vlogs REALLY love vlogs and desperately want them to continue daily. It is a lot of pressure to keep up with daily uploads. For me, another downside to vlogging is that you are exposing yourself to more criticism and scrutiny than a regular sit-down or one-topic video might bring. Even when you only show 10 minutes out of a 24-hour day, viewers start to assume that they know everything about you and can either be overly friendly (i.e., a bit like a stalker!) or too critical.

Most daily vloggers start out interacting with viewers in the comments but stop doing so as their subscribers increase because they feel the need to guard their privacy more closely. If vlogging interests you, consider starting by doing it once a week. You can always expand to more frequent vlogs if you decide you really enjoy doing them and do not feel like you are exposing too much of your personal life.

PRO TIP: Be sure to choose a category and theme for your channel that you love. Don't get swept up in trends. If you have fast food, you aren't going to be successful at making fast food review videos. If you have no interest in makeup, you aren't going to be happy trying to be a part of the beauty community. Search YouTube for topics you are interested in to see what types of videos are already out there. Try becoming a part of a community first by interacting with other people's videos. Then when you are ready to launch your channel, you will hopefully have some online friends to encourage you on your journey.

CHAPTER EIGHT: MAKING MONEY FROM GOOGLE ADSENSE

So far, in this book, I have already discussed how you make money on YouTube via AdSense; but there are other ways you can bring in even more income with your videos. While AdSense will be your first money-making stream, it will likely not be your last as you grow your channel. And the more your channel grows, the more income opportunities will present themselves to you.

In fact, the largest YouTube channels make most of their money from sources other than AdSense. For example, YouTuber Jeffree Star referred to his AdSense money as "extra" income on top of his multi-million-dollar beauty empire! And while you may not reach the level of fortune that Star has, you still have the potential to earn money on YouTube. From a bit of extra cash to a full-time level income, the possibilities of making money on YouTube are limitless!

ADSENSE: At the beginning of this book, I covered the basics for monetizing your videos with AdSense, which you do as part of the YouTube Partner Program. But you must understand how AdSense works and how you can best utilize it on your channel to maximize your earnings.

AdSense is the route by which Google sells advertising. You have likely seen Google-branded pop-up ads on various websites. The money that advertisers pay for those ads is processed through AdSense. When you are monetized on YouTube, Google will run ads on your videos; just like ads that appear on text-based websites, the ads that appear on videos are purchased and sold through AdSense. You can think of Google Ads and AdSense as being the same.

Whether on a website or in a YouTube video, the Google ads shown to you have matched the content you are reading or watching. For instance, if you are reading a travel article, you will likely see ads for Disney World or the various cruise lines. If you watch business-related videos, you'll be shown videos from other channels that create business content.

The same is true for the YouTube videos you watch. These ads are created and paid for by advertising companies. These companies pay Google to run the ads, and Google then splits the money with the content creators, both on blogs and websites as well as on YouTube. If you are creating beauty videos, then logically, the makeup companies that run Google ads will be interested in placing their ads on your videos.

How much you will earn via Google AdSense depends on several different factors, such as the type of ads placed on your videos, how viewers respond to the ads, and the cost that each particular advertiser is paying Google to run their ads. The more a brand pays for an ad, the more you will make if people watch your video. October through December, also referred to as the "4th quarter" is the busy holiday retail season, which means advertisers spend more on ads. In January, the ads drop off. Ad rates are seasonal, following the retail calendar.

On YouTube, how much money a video makes is first determined by the **CPM**. CPM stands for **cost per 1,000 impressions**, and the CPM is what YouTube can charge advertisers for ads placed on your videos. While you are not paid the CPM amount, it is essential to determine your **RPM**, which is your revenue cut, or revenue per 1,000 miles.

Again, CPM stands for what Google charges advertisers, and RPM is what Google pays you.

CPMs can be as low as 50 cents and as high as hundreds of dollars per one thousand views; it all depends on the video's content. Remember, the CPM is the amount of money YouTube charges advertisers, not the amount you are paid. Your RPM is usually half of your CPM, so a high CPM typically results in a high RPM.

The average price per view is less than 20 cents, meaning the average video earns around $18 per 1,000 views. Creators earn roughly 50% off the CPM, meaning the average YouTube creator is paid around $9 per 1,000 views. But remember that this is average; some people earn a lot more while others earn much less.

As a YouTube creator, you are paid per 1,000 views on all your videos combined throughout the month. For example, my general lifestyle videos sometimes earn $24 CPM per 1,000 views, making my cut $12 per 1,000 views. However, on average, my dedicated business videos can earn as much as $40 CPM per 1,000 views, making my share $20 per 1,000 views.

Why the difference? Well, lifestyle videos are a dime a dozen on YouTube; there is so much competition in this category that content creators end up splitting the share of advertising between thousands of different channels. However, e-commerce is a tiny, niche category, but one with a loyal viewer base. And it is an audience that is specifically interested in money-making opportunities.

While finance companies will not find their audience on makeup tutorial videos, they will find them on videos about eBay, Amazon, and Poshmark. Therefore, Google can charge those advertisers more as their audience is small. And since the reselling community, which is the community of those who sell on sites like eBay and Poshmark, on YouTube is relatively small, those of us who make reselling videos split the advertising dollars with fewer creators, making the CPM rates on our videos higher, thus resulting in higher RPM payouts. While there are hundreds of thousands of makeup tutorial videos, there may be less than 100 videos about how to list items for sale on Poshmark.

Bottom line: Niche content may not get as many views, but the advertising rates tend to be much higher, meaning your chances of earning money with a small audience are also much higher. Niche categories are also easier to break into. There are tens of thousands of gaming channels but not as many business channels. Even if your content falls under one of the larger categories, try to narrow it down by focusing on a specific topic.

For example, maybe you would focus on baking instead of a general cooking channel. Or rather than crafting, you would produce videos related to one specific crafting method, such as jewelry making. There are many types of products you can sell on Etsy, but the top YouTube Etsy creators focus on one type of business model to make videos on, which means they will earn top dollar from ads placed on their videos.

I have been fortunate that my CPMs have been on the higher side throughout my YouTube career. But my CPMs are constantly changing, going up and down depending on the money advertisers are investing in YouTube ads for the videos I make. As I mentioned earlier, the ad rates increase during price retail seasons such as Christmas and back-to-school.

Once your YouTube videos are monetized to earn AdSense revenue, you can track your CPM in your account's **YouTube Studio** area. Simply click on the **Analytics** tab on the left side of the page to see your AdSense totals (you can customize the date range), and then click on **Revenue** to see your CPM.

I personally like to check my numbers once a week to see how my month is going. Note that the data can be delayed and that you won't know exactly how much money you have earned until Google reconciles your account shortly before they issue your payout, which is the month following the month you earned AdSense in (for example, the money you made in January will be paid to you in February).

However, while your CPM number is important, it is your RPM, which stands for **Revenue Per Mile**, which is the amount of money you are actually earning. This metric represents how much money YouTube is paying you per 1,000 video views via Ads, Channel Memberships, YouTube Premium revenue, Super Chats, and Super Stickers (I will discuss each of these further in this chapter).

CPM is the cost per 1000 ad impressions BEFORE YouTube takes its cut.

RPM is your total revenue per 1000 views AFTER YouTube takes its cut.

When I look at my analytics on YouTube, the number I home in on is my RPM, as that is what YouTube is paying me for every 1,000 views. However, it's important to remember that your CPM and RPM fluctuate almost daily. Therefore, you want to focus on your average numbers.

While your CPM is an advertiser-focused metric that only includes income from the monetized ads on your videos, RPM is a creator-focused metric that provides for total revenue reported from all available sources. It also includes the total number of views from your videos. Your RPM number will always be lower than your CPM number as it is calculated after YouTube's revenue share and because it includes all views, even those on videos that, for whatever reason, were not monetized.

Confused? Do not worry; most people are! Google is data-driven and gives YouTube creators a lot of numbers. But remember that it's your RPM that is most important as that is the money you are making.

To be honest, I myself rarely dig too deeply into these numbers. I focus on tracking my revenue share in the **YouTube Studio section** of my YouTube account (simply click on your profile picture on the top right-hand side of your YouTube account and select *YouTube Studio* from the menu to find yours). By clicking on the **Analytics** icon on the left-hand side of the page, you can bring up your **Channel Analytics**. From here, you can see your current revenue and several other statistics. You can also choose the date range, including:

- Last seven days
- Last 28 days
- Last 90 days
- Last 365 days
- Lifetime
- Current year
- Previous year
- Each of the past three months
- Custom

As I mentioned earlier, I personally narrow my display screen to the current month to see how my revenue is tracking for that particular month. Selecting any of the time options will narrow down your statistics to an overview page where you can see your **Views, Watch time (hours), New subscribers,** and **Estimated revenue.**

I like to narrow down my numbers by clicking on the **Revenue** tab to see my RPM and CPM. Through red arrows, YouTube will also show you whether your numbers are up or down from the previous time frame. My running tally of revenue for the month lets me know how I am doing and maybe where I need to improve, whether it is by changing the title or thumbnail. If I see that similar-themed videos aren't performing as well as others, I may make the decision not to make videos on that topic anymore.

That being said, as I mentioned earlier, it's important to note that the reporting of these numbers does lag a bit. You will need to wait until the end of the month when YouTube finalizes your revenue report to see what you actually earned. Sometimes the number I see at the end of the month is higher when I get paid. However, I still like to check my numbers to get an idea of where I am.

Further down the page under **Revenue** are even more helpful insights and statistics, including your estimated revenue for each of the past six months, along with your top-performing videos via revenue for the current month. Noting your top-performing videos will show you what type of content your audience is reacting to, which will help you decide what videos to produce in the future.

You can also access your **Reach statistics,** such as impressions, clicks-through rates, views, and unique views. Under **Engagement**, you will find your watch time in hours and your average view duration. And finally, under **Audience**, you can see your unique viewers, average views per viewer, and the number of new subscribers.

Your subscriber count will go up and down, some days more than others. People are constantly leaving YouTube while new people are joining. And some people unsubscribe and resubscribe to channels regularly. You just hope that your numbers increase faster than they decrease. And while some people seem to gain subscribers very quickly, most channels grow more slowly. It can be hard not to compare yourself to others, but it's important to keep focused on your own YouTube journey.

All of these numbers, percentages, and statistics can be overwhelming. But the good thing is that you do not have to pay attention to them unless you enjoy digging through data. As I said, I only focus on my current running revenue balance and my CPM and RPM. In truth, it is only my RPM number and my running total of AdSense that is of any importance, as that is how much money I will be paid. When it's all said and done, the only real number that matters is the amount deposited into my bank account!

Oh, and when does YouTube pay you? **Once you have earned at least $100 via Google AdSense, Google will initiate a payment to you the following month.** So, if you earn $100 or more in January, you will get paid your January AdSense revenue in February, typically during the third week of the month. The money will carry over to the next month if you don't earn enough monthly to qualify for a payout. So, if you earned $50 in January, that $50 would carry into February. If you earned $60 in February, your total would then be $110, which you would receive in April. Your money will be deposited into the bank account you entered when you created your account.

Remember that **if you earn $600 or more from AdSense in a year, YouTube will provide you with a 1099 form** to submit with your taxes. YouTube will notify you if you have a tax form available, which you can then print out from your Google AdSense account page. But even if you don't receive a tax form, you will still need to report your earnings to the IRS. I will be going over YouTube accounting in the next chapter.

CHAPTER NINE: EARNING MONEY FROM AFFILIATE LINKS

While AdSense is the primary way most people earn money on YouTube, another way to bring in cash from your videos is through affiliate links. When you sign up to be an affiliate with a company, you can access affiliate links that will pay you a commission whenever someone buys an item through your personal link.

Amazon offers the most popular referral program, which I've already referenced numerous times, called **Amazon Associates.** This is the main program that most YouTubers use, as well as bloggers and social media influencers. I have been an Amazon Associate even before starting my YouTube channel, as I would share my links via my other social media accounts. I then utilized the program on my blog. And today, I use the program in a Facebook group I have devoted to deals and freebies, as well as on my business Facebook page and on Twitter.

To sign up for an Amazon Affiliate account, visit **affiliate-program.amazon.com.** By signing up as an Amazon Associate, you can create referral links to any of the products on Amazon's website. Then if you use or mention a product in your video and provide a link to it in your YouTube video description box, you will earn a commission if anyone goes through your link to purchase that product. If you show anything in your video that can be purchased on Amazon, you will want to link it underneath your video. Check out videos of large YouTubers and the links in their description boxes to see how people utilize these links.

However, it is important to note that the person who clicks on your link does not have to purchase the exact product you link to; you will earn a commission on ANY items they buy once they are on Amazon's site if they got there using your referral link. This enables creators to maximize their affiliate earnings.

Let's say you link a teapot that you showed in your video, and someone clicks on it. They are taken to Amazon's site where the teapot is listed. However, the key is that they don't have to buy the teapot. Amazon will track all their purchases over the next 24 hours, crediting you with *anything* they buy. And most people shop on Amazon a lot, meaning there is a good chance they will shop using your link.

One year I made several hundred dollars as people used my Amazon Associates links to buy new televisions during the holidays. I didn't even link to any televisions! But somehow, when people clicked on the products I linked, they ended up purchasing TVs during those 24 hours.

With Amazon being the largest e-commerce site globally, it makes sense that most YouTube creators are also Amazon Associates, as it is an easy way to earn additional money. Savvy YouTubers link the most expensive products they use, such as camera equipment. Didn't I tell you earlier in the book to check out large YouTube channels to see what camera equipment they used? Those folks are making a lot of money with those affiliate links!

The first link under my videos is to my Amazon storefront, which is a perk offered when you apply and are accepted as an Amazon Influencer. According to Amazon, "The Amazon Influencer Program is an extension of the Amazon Associates (affiliate) program, that brings product-related content from Influencers onto Amazon to help customers research and discover products they might be interested in. An influencer is anyone who has a meaningful social media following. Influencers across any category can participate in this program. Currently, you must have a YouTube, Instagram, TikTok, or Facebook account to qualify."

To see if you qualify, visit **affiliate-program.amazon.com/influencers.**

This unique "influencer" Amazon Associate storefront gives me a dedicated page on Amazon where I can organize all of the products I offer. In addition to the books, I write under my own name, I also create journals, planners, and notebooks that I sell on Amazon under the "Jean Lee" publishing name. Plus, I have a section for reselling supplies I use and a section for the home products I often show in my vlogs.

I can easily direct viewers to this one link if they want to check out my books and other items. And I can quickly delete or add new items at any time.

However, you do not need to be an Amazon Influencer to create lists of recommended products on Amazon or simply link them individually to earn money as an Amazon Associate.

In addition to the Amazon Associate program, there are all kinds of companies that offer affiliate opportunities. In addition to Amazon, you can sign up for FREE to be an affiliate with:

Adobe: Apply at adobe.com/affiliates.html. The Adobe Affiliate Program allows you to earn commissions when you promote Adobe Creative Cloud, Adobe Stock, and Adobe Document Cloud on your website, blog, or social media channels. Since these are programs that many social media creators use, these are logical products you may be able to promote.

Audible: Apply at audible.com/ep/affiliate-intro. Earn advertising fees when you refer viewers to qualifying Audible audio books, products, and memberships.

Brandcycle: Apply at brandcycle.com. Brandcycle allows influencers to partner with over 500 retail brands to access premium commission rates and exclusive offers. Stores include Kate Spade, Macy's, Old Navy, Wayfair, Coach, Carter's, and Nordstrom Rack.

eBay Partner Network: Apply at partnernetwork.eBay.com. Earn money by driving traffic and promoting sales across eBay, which is easy to do if you sell or buy on the site.

Honey: joinhoney.com/business/get-started. Earn money through this money-saving browser extension. Honey is also a popular sponsor of YouTube channels.

Movavi: Apply at movavi.com/partners/affiliate-program. Earn money promoting the Movavi video software, which is popular among some YouTubers.

Rakuten (formerly LinkShare): Next to Amazon Associates, Rakuten is arguably the most popular affiliate program. Apply at rakutenadvertising.com/affiliate. Rakuten has a shopping portal, formerly called Ebates, that pays users a percentage back on their purchases. Shoppers simply create a free Rakuten account and search the site for the retailer they want to shop from. They then click through to the store's website via Rakuten's link.

Rakuten automatically tracks their spending, giving them a percentage back of their total purchase amount (anywhere from 1% up to 20%, depending on the site). Every three months, Rakuten automatically mails users out rebate checks. There are no points to track or special codes to enter; the entire process is automated on Rakuten's end.

While I use Rakuten for my shopping rebates, I also use their affiliate program to make money. When you sign up for a Rakuten account, you are also given your own affiliate link to share on social media, including YouTube. When someone signs up for Rakuten using your affiliate link and makes a purchase, you then earn $25.

Any affiliate income you make from Rakuten is added to your rebate total, and a check is mailed out to you every three months. It is a safe, easy, and effective program to increase your overall YouTube earnings. And it is why you will see Rakuten affiliate links in many YouTube description boxes.

Shopify: Apply at shopify.com/affiliates. Earn commissions through your own Shopify store or by promoting others. Some YouTubers who sell their merchandise do so through a Shopify store. It's also a popular platform for those with their e-commerce businesses.

Sellfy: Apply at sellfy.com/affiliates. Earn commissions by bringing customers to the Sellfy website, which allows users to create their e-commerce platform.

ShareASale: Apply at shareasale.com/info. Earn money by promoting partner offers and brands from over 6,000 businesses with an average of 260 new merchants launching each month.

ShopHer Media: Apply at shophermedia.com/partners. Earn commissions by directing shoppers to the various ShopHer brands. You can link directly to products on multiple websites including Target, Walmart, Lowes, and many more.

ShopStyle Collective: Apply at shopstylecollective.com. Earn money by sharing links to products you love. ShopStyle has thousands of brands available to promote, especially those under the beauty and fashion categories.

Skillshare: Apply at skillshare.com/affiliates. Earn $7 for every new customer you refer to Skillshare, a website that hosts online classes and video lessons. Skillshare does a lot of YouTube channel sponsorships with individual creators, too.

TripAdvisor: Apply at tripadvisor.com/affiliates. Partner with the world's largest travel site to earn 50% commissions for providing hotel booking links.

Twitch: Apply at affiliate.twitch.tv. Twitch is an affiliate network specifically targeted toward streaming content.

CHAPTER TEN: MAKE MONEY WITH REFERRAL LINKS

While affiliate programs pay you in cash, referral programs reward you with products or credits for paying for your purchases. For example, for a while, I subscribed to numerous subscription boxes, which I reviewed on my YouTube channel. If the company had a referral link, I would provide the link in the video's description box. Then, I earned rewards if someone signed up for the subscription using my link. Sometimes it was points toward free products; other times, it was free boxes or products.

Since affiliate programs pay in cash, I generally prefer them over referral links. However, some companies offer both; it is then up to me to decide which reward is better. In some cases, I use the affiliate link to earn cash; in other cases, I may use the referral link to earn free products. It all depends on the reward.

For instance, I have a subscription to BarkBox, a monthly subscription box filled with treats and toys for dogs. They have both an affiliate program and a referral program. I choose to use my referral link as I earn points towards free boxes as my dogs love the products and it saves me money from paying out of pocket. For me, the credits are more valuable than the affiliate money I could earn, even though the affiliate percentage is higher than the referral credit.

Nowadays, nearly every brand and service offer a referral program, including major airlines and hotels, clothing and beauty companies, subscription boxes, and membership services. I belong to numerous referral programs, including FabFitFun, IPSY, and Thrive Marketplace, to name a few.

Whenever you show an item of your own in a video, say a piece of clothing or a kitchen accessory, visit the brand's website to see if they offer an affiliate or referral program so that when you link the product in your video, you will have the potential to earn either cash or credit. If you have a blog or website, you can also put ads from these companies on your site to earn credits and free products that way.

Some popular referral programs are as follows. A simple Google search for each company name followed by "referral program" will take you directly to the pages to sign up. You may find that some will lead you to the affiliate programs listed in the previous section, but some will have their own dedicated program.

A simple Google search of each of the following companies will take you to their websites. To find their referral programs, scroll down to the bottom of each page and look for links to sign up.

Acorns: This financial investment service specializes in micro-investing and robo-investing. Customers and those they refer receive a $5 bonus upon successfully setting up an account.

Airbnb: Earn up to $30 in credits when you refer someone who completes a reservation as a guest or a host.

American Express: If you have an American Express account, you can earn Membership Rewards for every successful referral.

American Giant: American Giant's tagline is "best hoodies in the world." Customers who successfully refer friends earn $20, while the referrals get a 15% discount.

Amerisleep: This natural memory foam mattress company will reward you with a prepaid Visa gift card when referrals order a mattress through your link.

Backcountry: This outdoor clothing seller offers both you and your referrals $10 toward future purchases.

Blinds.com: This custom window treatment retailer gives both the referrer and the referral recipient $20 on all orders.

Boden: This clothing retailer has a large online presence. You can earn a $15 credit when someone purchases through your link. The referral will receive 20% off their first purchase.

Brooklinen: This sheet and linen company offers several ways to earn credit, such as following them on social media and leaving reviews. Customers and referrals each receive 25% off their purchase of $100 or more.

Canva: This popular digital graphic design site gives customers credits toward premium images when their referral creates an account and completes a design.

Casper: Casper is an online mattress company that offers a rotating offer of referral credit offers, such as Amazon gift cards. The referred customer receives 20% off their order.

Chase: Chase offers online banking and credit cards. Users can earn between 5,000 and 10,000 points (equal to $50 and $100, respectively) when they refer friends and family.

Choice Hotels: Earn points toward future hotel stays when referrals complete a stay with a participating hotel.

Discover: Both customers and those they refer can earn statement credits via their referral program.

Dropbox: This online data storage service upgrades customers' storage for every referral they make.

eBags: This online luggage store gives customers $10 in reward points for every referral. Referrals get 65% off their first order.

Everlane: This online clothing retailer gives customers $25 credit for every successful referral.

FabFitFun: As I mentioned earlier, I subscribe to the FabFitFun subscription box, which means I am given referral codes to share. I earn $15 in referral credits for everyone who signs up using my link. The referrals receive $10 off their first box.

Fabletics: This Kate Hudson-founded company offers a fitness wear subscription. Subscribers are given a referral link that gives new customers 50% off their first order. For every friend you refer, you earn $10 in-store credit.

Farm Fresh To You: This organic fruit and vegetable delivery service gives customers a unique Refer-A-Friend link to share that gives referrals $15 toward their first order. In return, you receive a $25 credit.

Fiverr: Earn credit to use on your own Fiverr orders for everyone you refer so purchase a gig. I use Fiverr for some business graphics, so this is a useful referral program if you need help creating YouTube banners and social media posts.

Getaround: Called the Airbnb of car sharing, referral users earn $20 credit for anyone who signs up using their link.

Girlfriend Collective: This activewear brand sells clothes from recycled materials and offers a pair of free leggings when someone uses your referral link to make a purchase. The referrals are given $10 off their purchase of $95 or more.

Glossier: This online cosmetics company awards you with $10 in-store credit when a referred customer clicks on your link, creates an account, and places an order. The referrals receive 10% off their first purchase.

Google Workspace: The online work collaboration platform pays from $8 to $23 depending on the number of users you refer.

Groupon: Groupon is a deal site that offers discounts on products and services, both online and locally. Users can earn $10 in Groupon Bucks for every referral that purchases a Groupon.

Hanna Anderson: This children's apparel company gives customers 20% off a future order when referring friends and family. Referrals receive 20% off their first order.

HelloFresh: This meal subscription service rewards customers with a $20 credit for every successful referral. The referral gets $40 off their first box.

HotelTonight: Earn money toward your next booking when you share your referral link.

Hunter: Hunter makes pricey boots and outerwear. You can earn $15 per referral when they make a purchase. The referral gets $15 off their first order.

Ibotta: This popular shopping rebate app awards you $10 for everyone you refer who makes a purchase.

Intuit QuickBooks: Earn a $100 pre-paid Visa card for every person who subscribes through your link.

IPSY: This popular beauty subscription box rewards you with points for referring friends and reviewing products. The points can be redeemed for free makeup and skin care.

Lyft: Another popular ridesharing program, Lyft rewards when someone uses their referral link. You can choose cash, Lyft credit, or a combination of the two.

Madison Reed: This hair care company has a "share the love" program where you can earn a $15 credit for every referral that signs up using your link. The referrals receive a $15 discount on their first purchase.

Marriott Hotel: Earn up to 50,000 bonus points when you refer up to five new customers per year.

Minted: This online stationery company offers users $25 in credit when someone they refer purchases $100 or more. The referral also receives $25 off their first order.

Moo: This online print and design company offers two ways to earn rewards through referrals. When you refer a friend, they have the potential to win a $20 gift card. If you refer a business with a minimum of 10 employees, the reward increases to $150. The referrals themselves get 24% off their first order.

Naturebox: An online healthy snack shop that rewards customers with $10 off future orders for every friend they refer. Your referral link offers people 50% off their first order.

Outdoor Voices: Earn $20 to spend at this activewear retailer for every referral who signs up. The people you refer get 20% off their first order.

Peapod: This online grocery store allows you to share your referral link on social media or via email. Your link offers people $50 off their first two orders. In return, you will receive $25 toward your next order.

Rebecca Minkoff: This luxury women's retailer has a Refer-A-Friend program that gives both you and the referral $20 for each successful referral.

Robinhood: This online investment app rewards you and your referrals with free stock of up to $500 a calendar year.

Quip: Quip is a subscription-based dental company that provides customers with electric toothbrushes, refill packs, toothpaste, and dental floss. Earn $5 in credits for every referral you make. The referrals also earn $5 credit for every successful purchase they make. Quip also rewards you with $5 in credit when you invite your dentist to join.

Seated: This restaurant reservation app gives customers and those they refer credits to apply toward future reservations. When you have five successful referrals, you will be upgraded to "Seated Partner," where you can earn bonus rewards.

Shoes for Crews: This online store sells slip-resistant footwear to the workforce. Referrals reward both individuals with a $10 credit.

SoFi: This personal finance app offers six different referral programs, but the one on the app is the easiest. The app referral program awards you 2,000 points for everyone you refer, which equals $20 that you can apply to their checking, saving, or investment account options.

Swagbucks: One of the first points-based rewards companies offers customers gift cards and cash for completing activities online. Their referral program awards you 10% of whatever your referrals earn.

Thinx: This online retailer has a strong focus on women's health. Customers receive $10 for every customer they refer, and referrals are given $10 off their first order.

Timberland: Timberland sells rugged shoes and boots. You can earn 20% off your future purchase when someone you refer makes a purchase. The referrals also receive 20% off their first order.

Uber: The popular ride-share company rewards you with discounts and free rides when people sign up using your link.

Uniglo: This Japan-based clothing retailer gives customers $10 for every successful referral. The referrals receive $10 off their first order.

Verizon: If you are a Verizon customer, you can utilize their Refer-A-Friend program to earn up to $100 on a prepaid Mastercard when you successfully refer a new customer.

Vistaprint: This online print company sells various custom stationery products. Customers receive $10 when they successfully refer a new customer.

Vonage: Vonage is a "voice over internet protocol" service provider. Customers earn a $50 gift card for every referral who signs up for their service.

Winc: An online wine subscription service gives you two complimentary bottles of wine when anyone uses your link to place an order. The referral will also receive $22 of wine with their first purchase.

CHAPTER ELEVEN: GET RICH WITH SPONSORSHIPS

In addition to earning money through AdSense, Amazon Associates, affiliate links, and referral links, you can also bring in cash through sponsorships. A sponsorship is when a company pays you to film a video. If a company has a product to promote, they will send you the item and pay you to film a video about it. If it is a service, the company will pay you to talk about their company.

Large YouTube channels almost all make more money from sponsorships than they do from AdSense. When you look at the wealthy creators, they usually got rich from sponsorships. Not that they don't make a lot of money from AdSense; they do. But it's being paid by brands directly that brings in the most money.

I've accepted sponsorships from individual brands and websites. As my channel has grown, so has my ability to charge more for these sponsorships. The more subscribers a channel has, the more lucrative sponsorships can be. It takes a while to build up a large enough audience to attract sponsors; I began receiving sponsorship offers when my channel hit 5,000 subscribers (although I started getting offers of free products when my second channel barely had 1,000 subscribers). But it depends on what kind of content you are producing and how many actual views your videos typically get. Most brands will judge your channel based on your videos' average views, not necessarily by your subscriber numbers.

Note that you need to disclose sponsored videos, both verbally within the video and in the video's description box. If you look in description boxes under videos, many creators, including myself, include something along the lines of "This is not a sponsored video. All products were purchased with my own money and all opinions are my own."

However, if the video is sponsored, the language will change to something like, "This video is sponsored by ABCompany." There is also a box you much check when you are uploading a video to indicate whether or not you are receiving compensation.

While most sponsorships come from companies contacting creators directly, you can also sign up with sponsorship companies to connect you with potential sponsors.

A simple Google search for each of the following will take you to their websites where you can proceed with registration:

AspireIQ: Formerly called Revfluence, AspireIQ markets itself as the leading influencer marketing platform. They connect brands with influencers, paying creators to create content that drives traffic to the companies they represent, including Bed Bath & Beyond, Marriott, Walmart, and Nike. In addition to YouTube, you can also earn money from them on your blog/website, Facebook page, Twitter feed, and even Pinterest. Learn more at aspireiq.com.

Channel Pages by FanBridge: Channel Pages has no minimum YouTube subscriber count to qualify for signing up. They have an extensive collection of brands, both big and small. Their platform lets you connect with brands and apply for collaboration opportunities with other channels. Learn more at channelpages.com.

Content BLVD: Content BLVD works with cosmetics brands such as Urban Decay and Skin & Co. Content BLVD works exclusively with YouTubers who are paid to review the brands they represent. Not only can you get free products, but you will also be paid to make a video about them. Learn more at contentblvd.com.

Grapevine: Grapevine works with influencers with 10,000 YouTube subscribers or 10,000 Instagram followers. However, even if you haven't reached that level of followers, you can still sign up with them.

They help you choose brand deals based on your channel size, niche, and demographics. Some companies they work with are Walgreens, NYX, and Remington. Learn more at grapevinevillage.com.

Izea: There are no minimum subscriber counts in order to sign up with Izea, a company that works to connect food, fashion, beauty, and lifestyle brands with content creators. Some of the companies they represent include Subway, Levi's, and EBay. They also offer freelancing gigs. Learn more at izea.com.

TapInfluence: TapInfluence has no minimum subscriber requirement and can connect you with food, fashion, beauty, and lifestyle brands such as WhiteWave Food, MtoM Consulting, and Stella & Chewy's. Their "open bidding" feature lets you bid on projects that match your content. Learn more at tapinfluence.com.

YouTube Brand Connect: Formerly called Famebit, the newly rebranded YouTube Brand Connect offers YouTube creators sponsorships for big brands, including Canon, Sony, and Adidas. YouTube Brand Connect is currently invite-only for channels with 25,000 subscribers. If you become eligible, YouTube will notify you within your YouTube Studio interface.

Note that the companies listed above are not the only places to obtain sponsorships, as some brands work independently to connect with creators. Once you start gaining subscribers, you will likely start to be contacted directly by companies who either want to send you free products to review or who are willing to pay you a sponsorship fee for mention in a video.

A critical part of getting YouTube sponsorships is settling on the amount of money you expect to be paid. If you are just starting out on YouTube, you cannot expect a company to pay you thousands of dollars to sponsor a video. In fact, in the early days of your YouTube career, you may only be able to film videos in exchange for free products.

However, as your channel grows, you can start to expect payment for your services. Most brands will try to pay you as little as possible, if anything at all, so, you must go into YouTube with the mindset that your time is valuable. If a company approaches you with a sponsorship offer, it is because they feel you are a good fit for their brand. Therefore, they should already expect that they will need to pay you to film a sponsored video for them.

While sponsors look at your total subscriber count, they also examine how many views your videos average. Only you can answer how much you will be comfortable charging, although a good formula to start with is $0.05 to $0.15 per view or $50 to $150 per 1,000 views. Some brands ask you for your rate, while others propose a fixed price. In the end, only you can decide the rate you will charge.

You must have policies in place before accepting a sponsorship deal. You want to agree on:

1. When will the video go live?
2. How long will the video need to be in terms of length?
3. Does the brand need to approve the video before it launches?
4. When and how will you receive your payment?
5. Will the company be providing you with a script?
6. Will the company provide links and discount codes to share with your viewers?
7. Will you be given free products to show in your video?
8. What else does the company expect from you? For example, will you be expected to share the video on social media?
9. Will the company require that you use specific hashtags?
10. Will the company provide disclosure text in the video's description box?

Some companies will ask very little of you other than filming a video discussing their product or service, while others will expect you to sign a contract and complete numerous steps to get paid. I have had some brands mail me a product to show in a video, while others have demanded I sign a contract with detailed instructions on how, what, where, and when to film. The more a company expects of you, the more you should expect from them in terms of compensation.

CHAPTER TWELVE: MONETIZING YOUR BRAND

A big part of building a successful YouTube career involves building a brand, even if you are the brand. While affiliate and referral links along with sponsorships bring in more money than just AdSense alone, you can earn even more money when you offer products based on your channel's identity.

MERCHANDISE: From tee shirts and coffee mugs to courses and books, YouTube creators frequently sell their own merchandise, also called "merch."

You can create your own branded merch and link it directly to your YouTube channel through YouTube's partnership with TeeSpring. According to TeeSpring, "This means that you can have your merchandise appear beneath your YouTube videos. Early data from a group of beta creators demonstrated that using the merch shelf led to a meaningful increase in visits to purchase pages as well as revenue from merchandise sales. We're excited to work with YouTube to diversify your income through merch and make it more accessible to your viewers on YouTube."

Visit **community.teespring.com/answers/youtube-integration-faqs** for more information.

Note that you can offer more merchandise through other sites such as TeePublic, Bonfire, Redbubble, and more. These sites "host" your product designs, printing products and shipping them directly to customers for you. You can hire designers on sites such as Fiverr to create designs for you.

I create my designs using Canva Pro software, which requires a small monthly fee. An app like WordSwag is free and easy to use for text-only designs. Or sites like Creative Fabric offer subscriptions to access graphics you can use for commercial use.

If you have a nickname or tagline, consider slapping it on a tee shirt or coffee mug and offering it up for sale to your YouTube viewers to help grow your brand and bring in extra money. I have friends who create new merchandise for every season. The TeeSpring option connected to your YouTube account makes adding merch easy. All you then do is collect your share of the profits.

CHANNEL MEMBERSHIPS: Channel memberships are a relatively new feature for YouTube creators. Memberships allow viewers to join your channel through monthly payments, enabling them to receive benefits such as special emojis, badges, stickers, and videos only offered to members.

Note that there is a minimum eligibility requirement that creators must meet before being able to apply to offer Channel Memberships. As of this writing, requirements include:

- Your channel must have more than 1,000 subscribers
- Your channel must be enrolled in the YouTube Partner Program
- You must be over 18 years of age
- You must be located in one of the eligible countries (Argentina, Australia, Austria, Bahrain, Belarus, Belgium, Bolivia, Bosnia and Herzegovina, Brazil, Bulgaria, Canada, Chile, Colombia, Costa Rica, Croatia, Cyprus, Czech Republic, Denmark, Dominican Republic, Ecuador, El Salvador, Estonia, Finland, France, Germany, Greece, Guatemala, Honduras, Hong Kong, Hungary, Iceland, India, Indonesia, Ireland, Israel, Italy, Japan, Kuwait, Latvia,

Lebanon, Liechtenstein, Lithuania, Luxembourg, Macedonia, Malaysia, Malta, Mexico, Netherlands, New Zealand, Nicaragua, Norway, Oman, Panama, Paraguay, Peru, Philippines, Poland, Portugal, Qatar, Romania, Russia, Saudi Arabia, Senegal, Serbia, Singapore, Slovakia, Slovenia, South Africa, South Korea, Spain, Sweden, Switzerland, Taiwan, Thailand, Turkey, Uganda, United Arab Emirates, United Kingdom, United States, Uruguay, Vietnam)
- Your channel has a Community Tab
- Your channel is not set as "made for kids"
- Your channel does not have a significant number of ineligible videos (such as set as being "made for kids" or with music claims)
- You are complying with YouTube's terms and policies

If you are eligible and choose to offer Channel Memberships to your viewers, you can select from several "perks" to features, including:

- Badges
- Emojis
- Private videos
- Live chats
- Downloads of content
- In-person meetings
- Contests
- Sweepstakes

Some creators also offer physical items they mail out to their channel members, such as stickers, cards, shirts, and more. You can offer memberships priced as low as $0.99 per month up to $99.99 a month. Creators receive 70% of membership revenue after applicable taxes, and fees are taken out.

YOUTUBE PREMIUM: YouTube Premium is a subscription service that costs $11.99 per month and allows viewers to:

- Watch videos ad-free
- Download videos to watch offline
- Play videos in the background while using other apps
- Access the YouTube Music App
- Listen to music ad-free
- Download music to listen to offline
- Play music in the background while using other apps
- Watch ad-free YouTube Kids videos as well as the ability to play offline
- Listen to Google Play Music (for most countries)

Creators do not have to subscribe to YouTube Premium for their videos to be included in the subscription. And while ads will not appear on your videos if someone with a YouTube Premium account is viewing them, you will still receive a cut of the membership fees that are being paid to YouTube by subscribed viewers.

SUPER CHATS & SUPER STICKERS: Super Chats and Super Stickers allow viewers to connect with creators during live chats. Viewers can purchase Super Chats to send creators money; their comment then appears highlighted in the chat. Viewers can also purchase Super Stickers, which is a digital or animated image that pops up in the live chat feed.

Channels with many subscribers can often earn quite a bit of money from viewers sending them these chats and stickers during live stream videos. For those with huge channels, a Super Chat is often the only way for a viewer to be noticed by a creator during a live stream, as the creator will hear a notification sound when they receive a donation, and the comment or sticker is highlighted in the chat stream.

PATREON: Patreon is a membership service that some YouTube creators utilize to earn additional income. Some channels use Patreon like a tip jar, while others have multiple membership levels, each with varying perks, such as exclusive videos and merchandise.

Patreon is a more profitable option than YouTube Memberships, as Patreon creators keep more of their profits. However, YouTube Memberships keep everything organized in your channel dashboard. It's a preference of the creator which they choose.

TIP JAR: Just as some creators use Patreon as a virtual tip jar, you can also collect tips on your blog, website, or YouTube channel in several ways, including by providing your audience with your PayPal, Stripe, or Venmo email. A simple message such as "If you would like to support my channel with a virtual tip, you can send it to" with the email address associated with your account.

SHORTS: TikTok creators have been making the leap to YouTube via Shorts, which are video clips no longer than one minute. Shorts can be monetized if you are already a YouTube Partner. If not, Shorts can be monetized after you have 1,000 subscribers and 10 million Shorts views within 90 days.

Shorts are a great way to not only increase your YouTube earnings but also your following as YouTube pushes these clips. TikTok creators can easily upload a 60-second TikTok to YouTube as a Short, monetize it, and make more money than the clip earned them on TikTok.

PRO TIP: Create a 60-second or less TikTok video. Post it on YouTube as a Short. Then share it on Instagram and Facebook as a Reel. With one short video, you have content for FOUR social media platforms!

CHAPTER THIRTEEN: YOUTUBE ACCOUNTING MADE EASY

As you start this chapter, I know what you might be thinking: "I want to start a YouTube channel, not worry about accounting!"

Well, that is the catch when it comes to making money online: Like it or not, you must pay taxes on the money you earn, and that includes what you earn on YouTube. While it would be great to keep all the AdSense and sponsorship money you earn every month, if you earn more than $600 in a year from your channel, you will be giving a cut to Uncle Sam every year.

And whether you want to track your income or not, in the end, the IRS will come for their share of the money. Google reports all earnings to Google, so the government knows if you've been cashing in on your videos. That goes for all of the money you make outside of Google AdSense, including sponsorships and affiliate marketing.

The good news is that YouTube bookkeeping is relatively easy. Unlike my eBay and Etsy businesses, where I have considerable expenses and forms to keep track of, it is much easier to manage my YouTube income and expenses. However, it is still important that I keep detailed records as there are tax write-offs associated with running my YouTube channel, which helps reduce my tax bill.

DISCLAIMER: Before I dive deeper into how I manage my YouTube bookkeeping, please note that I am not an accountant. I PAY an accountant to file my taxes for me. However, I do keep track of my income and expenses throughout the year. Be sure to consult with an accountant or tax professional in your area regarding your tax obligations. The following advice is just that: Advice.

INCOME: Now, even with an accountant handling my tax filing, I still need to provide him with my actual income numbers and channel expenses. I track my income and expenses throughout the year so that come tax time, I have my numbers ready to hand over to my accountant.

This system is the same as keeping a personal checking account register, although you will break down your expenses into specific categories. But the basics are as follows:

- You need to track your **GROSS INCOME**, also referred to as your **CREDITS**, which is the money you bring in.
- You then need to track your **EXPENSES**, also referred to as your **DEBITS**, which are the costs you can claim as deductions on your tax returns.

For example, every month, I record the following streams of income from my YouTube channel:

- **AdSense:** This is the money paid directly to YouTube creators from Google from the ads placed on videos. If you earn more than $600 in AdSense in a calendar year, Google will issue you a 1099 form. AdSense is deposited into my account around the third week of every month from the previous month's earnings.
- **Sponsorships:** Any money that a company pays you to promote their products/services on your channel. Most companies do not provide 1099 forms, so you will manually need to track this money.
- **Affiliates:** Any money earned from viewers buying something through an affiliate link. For example, I earn money on Amazon through my Amazon Associates links.
- **Free Product:** Talk to your account about reporting income

based on any free products you receive for review on your channel as laws vary.

Every year, Google sends me a 1099 form for the AdSense I earned from the ads on my channel. Remember that if you earn more than $600 in a year, Google will issue you a 1099 form. You can choose to have them mail the 1099 form to you, or you can print it off online. Do not worry: YouTube will notify you if and when your 1099 form is ready. They are pushing for creators to access the forms directly from their accounts, and the forms are accessible even after you print out a copy in case you need to go back in and print out more.

However, even if you do not meet the $600 threshold to receive a 1099 form, you still need to claim what you did earn from AdSense on your taxes. Be sure to consult with an accountant or tax professional in your area, as some states and countries have different rules than others. Any money you earn on YouTube, whether through AdSense, Memberships, or SuperChats, will be reflected on the same 1099 form as it all comes from Google.

As for sponsorships, it depends on the company if they send you a 1099 form. Many do not, but you still need to track that income. I have personally never received a 1099 form from a sponsor, but I have also never made a large amount of money from sponsorships. You will need to ask any company that sponsors you what their policy is. Be sure to note how you will be paid and if they will be issuing you a tax form before you sign a contract.

Patreon sends users 1099 forms if they earn $20,000 in a year. However, if you live in Illinois, they will issue you a 1099 form if you earn $1000 or more in a year. If you live in Maryland, Massachusetts, Vermont, or Virginia, the threshold to receive a 1099 form is $600 or more in a year. But like sponsorships, even if you do not receive a tax form, you will still need to claim any money you earn from Patreon. Again, check with a professional in your area, as the laws vary by state and country.

Some YouTube creators set up donation links, and while it may not amount to very much, you still need to account for it. And if you are selling merchandise through TeeSpring or any other website, you'll need to track that, too.

If you receive free products in exchange for reviewing them on your channel, you also may need to account for the monetary value of the items. Again, this is where you need to consult with a tax professional in your area to ensure you are following the specific rules in your state or country.

EXPENSES: After you have tallied your gross income total related to your YouTube channel, you next need to itemize your expenses. Since Google pays YouTube creators advertising royalties, YouTube is looked at as a business by the government. While this means you need to claim the money you make, it also means you can claim expenses as tax write-offs.

Expenses most YouTube creators claim, depending on the tax laws in their area, are as follows:

Bank Fees: It is wise to set up a separate bank account for any business you have, including YouTube. Most banks charge checking account fees, but credit unions typically do not. If you already have a bank account, it is okay to stick with that for now. But if you start earning a large amount of money on YouTube, you will definitely want to consider a dedicated account just for your channel earnings.

Phone/Internet: Your smartphone and internet connection are both essential for running your channel, meaning you can claim these as expenses. From the phone itself to the plan you are on, along with the internet connection you pay for, all are deductions you can claim on your taxes. If you are using your phone and internet for other things besides YouTube, you may be only able to claim a partial amount of the total bill.

Equipment: Even the most basic YouTube setup (um, that would be mine, ha-ha!) requires equipment. Cameras, tripods, lighting, computers, and printers are all business expenses you can claim as deductions. I order most of these items from Amazon, which makes it easy to track as I can simply look at my order records.

Software/Subscriptions: Paying for editing software and graphic subscriptions can add up. Fortunately, these are business deductions for YouTubers. Do not forget any apps you pay for, as you can claim those, too. I pay for all of these things using the same credit card, which makes tracking the costs as simple as I simply review my monthly statements.

Office Supplies: Copy paper, pens, and toner ink for your printer - these are all items you are likely using to manage your YouTube channel, so keep track of what you are spending on them.

Advertising: I occasionally run Facebook ads for my YouTube channel. Since I have a Facebook page, setting up advertisements on the site is easy. I also include business cards and any other promotional materials I buy in the "advertising" category.

Props: If you are spending money on your video backgrounds or buying things to show on camera, these items count as props, and you can claim them come tax time. Some tax professionals might recommend you add these costs under "Equipment."

Travel: If you travel at all for your channel, whether for a vacation vlog or to attend meetings or conventions related to content creation, you can usually claim expenses such as airfare and hotels. I once claimed a Disney World vacation because I was writing a book about it!

Meals: You can claim any money you spend on meals if you are doing so for your channel. For instance, maybe you are treating a fellow creator with whom you are collaborating out to lunch. Or perhaps you are reviewing a restaurant for your channel. Keep those receipts and write down how much you spend. Note that you can claim meals during business travel, but not usually food you eat during a regular day where you live, even if you are vlogging that day.

Taxes: As your channel grows, you may find that you are making enough money that you will need to pay quarterly income tax. Quarterly income tax is something many small businesses schedule to avoid paying one large lump sum at the end of the year. I pay both state and federal quarterly taxes four times a year. An accountant can set this up for you. Or, if you file taxes yourself, the IRS may mail you the forms for federal returns. Usually, you can have these forms generated for you to print using tax preparation software.

My accountant prepares the forms I need to mail in; all I have to do is write the checks and address the envelopes. This does not mean that I will not still owe taxes, but it helps with a big chunk of it. If I earn more than anticipated, I will then still owe come tax time. But if my income was down, I may end up with a refund. Taxes are unavoidable, so again, consult with an accountant!

Mileage: You may not think you are driving much for your YouTube channel, but you likely are. If you are a vlogger, you definitely are. But even if you only film sit-down videos at home, you are probably still driving a bit in relation to your channel. Whether it is going to a new local restaurant to film a review or driving to a big box store to purchase filming equipment, be sure to track your mileage as you may be able to deduct it come tax time. You can download several free apps to your smartphone to track your mileage. My favorite is MileIQ which tracks your miles just by the movement of your phone while in the car.

NET PROFIT: At the end of every month, add up your gross income numbers and then add up your expenses. Subtract your expenses from your total gross income to get your monthly NET PROFIT.

Then at the end of the year, tally up each individual category to get your year-end numbers. For example, add up the monthly totals for "Office Supplies" to get your total amount for the year. These total numbers of income and expenses are what your accountant will need to prepare your taxes.

See how it works just like a personal check register? You track the money coming in and the money going out. The only difference is that you want to itemize the money going out into different categories.

You can set up a system to track income and expenses using an Excel spreadsheet, or online accounting software, or you can use a notebook. I use a notebook and then transfer the numbers to a spreadsheet. How you track your numbers isn't important; the important thing is that you track them.

Having to hand over a chuck of your hard-earned money to the government is not fun for anyone, but it is a fact of life. And if you want to be successful on YouTube and make money on the site, you will have to deal with taxes. Find a good local accountant who understands small home-based businesses with 1099 forms to file along with deductions related to that business. The expense of a good accountant is worth it to have your taxes filed correctly!

CHAPTER FOURTEEN: PROMOTING YOUR YOUTUBE CHANNEL

If you want to establish a presence on YouTube and earn money from your videos, you will have to do everything you can to promote your channel and build your brand. YouTube is a social media platform, and you want to use all the other social media sites available to you to draw traffic to your videos. More traffic equals more views, which in turn equals more AdSense revenue, which can also lead to sponsorship opportunities as your channel grows.

Fortunately, the social media sites that will bring you the most traffic are all free and easy to use. And it is likely that you already have accounts on some or even all of them. Once you get into the habit of promoting your videos via social media, it becomes second nature and is a quick step to complete every time you upload a new video.

Setting up your various social networking sites is yet another reason why it is so essential that you choose the best YouTube channel name possible right out of the gate. You want to be known under the same name everywhere to establish your brand.

I am now "Ann Eckhart" on my main YouTube channel as well as on Facebook, Twitter, Instagram, TikTok, and Pinterest. I use the same profile photo across all my sites, too, so that no matter what website someone is browsing, when they see "Ann Eckhart" and my picture, they know it is me.

While I do YouTube for fun, it is also a business for me. Everything I create regarding my channel is done to promote it as a brand. My videos drive traffic to my books, and my books drive traffic to my channel. My social media sites promote both my books and my YouTube channel. And they all drive traffic to my eBay store and Etsy shops.

I call this my trifecta of promotion: YouTube, books, and social media all work together to drive traffic to each other, which grows my audience and results in more book sales, more eBay and Etsy sales, more affiliate income, more AdSense dollars, and more opportunities for sponsorships.

Whenever I get burned out on YouTube or discouraged because my channel isn't growing as fast as others, I remind myself that YouTube is just one piece of my entire business portfolio. Even if I didn't earn money from YouTube, I would still make videos as they are essentially free advertising for my other business ventures.

However, if you plan on YouTube being your only business, at least to start, you will still want to leverage the power of social media to grow your subscribers. Some creators seem to grow successful channels with little to no effort, while others struggle to get their channels off the ground. Most fall into the later scenario. The good news is that social media can help.

This chapter will cover all of the possible ways you can market your videos to grow your channel. Note that you do not have to do any of these if you do not want to, and you certainly do not have to do all of them. However, some social media promotion is beneficial in promoting your videos. So even if you are not currently using social media, give it a chance to grow your channel.

FACEBOOK: If you want to "brand" yourself and your YouTube channel, you will want to set up a Facebook page. YouTube makes it easy to share your videos on Facebook as a "share" button is located under all videos. Simply click on the Facebook icon, link your YouTube and Facebook accounts together, and you can then share your YouTube videos on your personal and/or business pages. And since Facebook now owns Instagram, you can harness the power of both sites with one post when you link your accounts together.

Note that while you may have a personal Facebook account, you will want to set up a Facebook PAGE for your YouTube channel. A Facebook business page differs from a personal Facebook page, although you first need to have a personal account and page to set up a business page.

A business page is one people "like," while a personal page is one where people "friend" you. A personal Facebook page limits the number of "friends" you can have, but you can have limitless "likes" on your business page. Plus, having a business page also allows you to separate your personal and public life.

My personal Facebook page is private and is only for my personal friends and family to see. However, my "Ann Eckhart" Facebook page is public; anyone can view it, "like" it, and "follow" it to see my posts. Since my public page is a business page, it also allows me to accept sponsorships from companies that pay me to post about their products on my feed.

As your YouTube channel grows, you will likely find that viewers want to "friend" you on your personal Facebook page. Even if you are not promoting your personal page, it will still be easy for most people to find. Unless it is a subscriber you have gotten to know very well, I strongly encourage you NOT to add subscribers as friends on Facebook. You want to maintain privacy with a division between your personal and public/business life.

While many of my friends and family "like" my Facebook business page, not all do. Keeping my personal page private protects me and my friends and family from exposing their information to my business page followers. You can try to "hide" your personal Facebook page by not using your photo in your profile picture and by using a different name, such as your first and middle name or a maiden name if you have one.

I use my Facebook business page to promote my YouTube videos and books and save my personal information for my personal Facebook account. While it is hard to turn down friend requests from well-meaning people, I only accept Facebook "friend" requests from my actual friends and family for safety and security reasons. YouTube subscribers and readers of my books need to "like" my Facebook business page to connect with me.

I have set up my personal Facebook page with the tightest security settings to protect myself. I have also turned off the private messaging settings on my business page so people cannot send me messages. When I allowed people to message me, I found myself inundated with long notes from people wanting advice on eBay, help with publishing a book, or just looking for someone to chat with. While most of these messages were harmless, it took a lot of my time and energy to deal with all the questions and to awkwardly minimize engaging with those who wanted to talk.

Again, just as it is hard to deny friend requests, it can be hard to ignore messages from well-meaning followers. However, I always remind myself that I am not just running my businesses, including my YouTube channel, for profit. In other words, I need the money to pay my bills! And while YouTube has never been my primary source of income, I am continuously growing my brand for the long term. Therefore, I treat everything I do as a business. I also must protect myself and my family by guarding my personal information as much as possible. Hence why I am very protective of my online privacy.

A Facebook page needs "likes" to grow. While it can take a while to build up the number of "likes" on a business page, I still believe setting one up separately from your personal account is essential. I have seen many people start out using their personal Facebook account for their online content, only to reach the maximum number of "friends" allowed eventually. They then had to scramble to create a business page and encourage everyone to "like" it. Facebook users are more accustomed to "friending" people than "liking" pages, so it does take longer to build a business page than a friend list.

To set up a free Facebook business page, visit **facebook.com/about/pages.**

You will need to log into your personal Facebook account first, and then the system will walk you through the steps necessary to create your business page. Creating a Facebook business page is free and easy to do, and I consider it an essential step in establishing your brand and building your YouTube channel.

The first decision you will need to make is to **name your business's Facebook page**. My Facebook business page is *Ann Eckhart*, the same name as my books and YouTube channel, not to mention the name I use on my other social media accounts. You will also want your page name to match your YouTube channel name.

As you create more social media accounts, you will want your name to be the same across all platforms. Remember, the goal is to create a brand of yourself so that people will recognize you on all forms of social media.

There are all kinds of things you can personalize on your Facebook page. You want to add a profile picture and a banner. I have a headshot as my profile picture, and I make my own customized banners for social media on apps like *Canva* and *WordSwag*. If you need help with graphics, you can hire designers for under $10 on a site like Fiverr.

Whatever photos or graphics you choose, remember that this is your BUSINESS page, so keep it professional. You do not want to post potentially controversial photographs of yourself; look at other YouTube creators' Facebook pages to get an idea of the kinds of photos and graphics that are acceptable to share.

You will also want to fill out the extensive **About** section of your page to provide people with information about your YouTube channel. However, since this is your BUSINESS page and separate from your personal page, you will want to be careful with how much information you share. While you may have your cell phone number available on your personal page to keep in touch with family and friends, unless you have a brick-and-mortar location that you want people to call, you will want to leave that section blank on your business page.

You will need to choose the **Category** for your page; as a YouTube creator, there are several categories you can choose from, such as "Public Figure," "Entertainer," or "Personal Blog or Website." I prefer the latter; please do not dub yourself a public figure or celebrity until you reach at least a million subscribers. Touting yourself as something other than you will turn off potential followers. "Entertainer" or "Entertainment" is less offensive than "Public Figure," in my opinion. If you are making videos about a niche topic, such as cooking, crafting, parenting, or travel, look for those categories.

In addition to your **Name** (the name of your page, i.e., your YouTube channel name), you can edit your Facebook URL so that it ends in that name. This provides you with a clickable URL link that you will want to provide on both your YouTube channel's "About" section and in the description box under all of your videos. The URL for my Facebook page is facebook.com/anneckhart.

PRO TIP: If you plan for YouTube to be your main business, consider buying a custom URL from a site such as GoDaddy.com to easily direct people to your channel. The main page I want to send people to my Amazon store where all of my books and recommended products are. Therefore, I purchased the URL AnnEckhart.com, which is much easier for people to remember than the longer Amazon-provided URL. Consider buying not only the .com URL but others such as org and info. And even if your channel is named something other than your legal name, consider buying the URLs for your name, too. After all, if you make it big on YouTube, you want to ensure you own any URLs related to you and your brand before someone else takes it!

Once you have created your Facebook business page, Facebook will prompt you to fill out all of the **Settings**, which you can choose to do at a later date or edit at any time in the future.

After you have your Facebook business page set up, it is time to start building your audience by getting people to "Like" your page. You will be able to invite friends and family on your personal page to "Like" your new business page. And, of course, you can promote your Facebook page on your YouTube channel by adding your page URL to the "About" section on YouTube and providing the link under all of your videos.

After all of your Facebook and other social media accounts are active, you will want to make sure to provide links to all your pages in the **About** information section of your YouTube channel home page, plus in the description box under each video. Note that you need to enter the full URL address of your sites, including the "http://" as only the complete "http" links will be active, allowing viewers to click through to the sites directly.

To make this process easy, I have my full description bar write-up and links in a Word document that I simply copy and paste into the description box of every video I upload. I will discuss this further in the chapter, *A Day in the Life of a YouTuber*, later in this book.

As I mentioned earlier, I ensure all my social networking accounts and websites work together to drive as much traffic as possible to my videos. When I upload a new YouTube video, I post the link to Facebook. Unfortunately, Facebook has made it increasingly difficult for people to see posts, hiding posts from business pages as they want those of us with pages to pay for the posts to be seen. This is frustrating, but there are some things you can do to help your posts be seen.

Once you have a business page and start posting there, you will likely notice the **Boost** buttons under posts that encourage you to pay for your updates to be directly shown to your followers. And while it can be tempting to spend $5 or more to ensure your posts are seen, resist the urge to boost everything you put on Facebook, as the results are not worth the cost. Instead, perhaps spend $5 every other week or so to promote one post to see if it affects your page "likes" and/or your YouTube subscriber growth.

I choose one video per month to "boost" on Facebook, typically one that is already performing well. You might be wondering why I would focus on a video that is already getting views. The reason is "low-hanging fruit." It is better to promote your best-selling products, in this case, a video that is performing well, in the hopes that it will bring people to your other products, in this case, the other videos on your channel.

I utilize this technique when I run ads for my books. I only advertise my bestsellers. These books sell well without advertising, but my books' sales increase when I advertise them. Why? Because if someone buys one of my books and enjoys it, they are likely to come back and purchase another of my titles. And since my best sellers are my best reviewed, I want to start them off with my best books.

The same is true for running ads on a well-performing YouTube video. If many people are organically finding and watching a particular video, it only makes sense that others will join in once they see it is popular.

Think about it like this: Say you saw an ad for a product with no reviews. Amazon products will show the number of stars a product has received, which indicates how popular an item is. You may get an ad for a product with no reviews, but then you get an ad for a product with thousands of reviews. When choosing between the two, most people will choose the product with the most reviews.

In the same way, on YouTube, viewers go with the videos with the most views. Let's say you search for "best vlogging camera" on YouTube. The results show you various videos that all look relatively the same. The only difference is the number of views they have. If you must choose one, will you watch the video with only a few dozen views or the video with thousands of views? I am betting that you choose the one that the most people have watched.

If you have a video that is performing well on YouTube, that is the one I would choose to "boost" on Facebook. Boosting a post turns your post into an ad that will be shown to the audience you specify. Facebook can target your ad to who they think will be the most interested in it, or you can narrow down your audience.

When I boost a post that features a YouTube video, I choose Facebook to target the people who "like" my page AND the people who are connected to them (the friends and family of the people who already "like" my page). You have likely seen ads in your Facebook feed and have noticed that the ad shows you which of your Facebook friends like that company. Seeing that your friends already like a company will make you more likely to click on the ad.

However, if you are new in your YouTube journey, you likely have very few people who "like" your page. In this case, I would recommend that you let Facebook choose the audience they will show the ad to. You can set a low budget – like I said, even just $5 – for a few days and see how it performs.

Because Facebook is selective about what posts they will show your followers, it is essential to do more than just post links to your Facebook page to engage your audience. Facebook prefers original posts and photos over links that you simply copy and paste to your page.

I try to post a regular status update at least once a day, which is more likely to be shown to my followers than a post with a link that I share directly from my blog. I also occasionally share photos on my Facebook page; like status updates, pictures tend to show up to more people than just links to my blog. Since my Facebook and Instagram accounts are linked, it is easy to share whatever I post to Instagram to Facebook. That way, I can knock out two social media posts in just one step.

Another way to engage your Facebook page users is to post "teasers" for upcoming videos. Post a photo of yourself as you are prepping to film or a picture of something you are getting ready to share, with the message that a new video will be coming the next day. This will get people excited about your latest video being released.

You want to encourage people to "like" and "comment" on your Facebook posts in the hopes their activity will show up on their friends' feeds, which will help more people come to your page. As I mentioned, for Facebook ads, you have likely seen this happen on your Facebook feed, where it will show you that a friend liked a post or a page. The convenient "like" thumbs-up icon will be there, making it easy for you to "like" the page.

I hope that when someone "likes" one of my posts, their friends will see it, check out my page, and then "like" it, too. As I mentioned earlier, Facebook shows status updates and photos more than links; so, I get more "likes" and comments on my status updates and pictures than I do when I simply share links to my blog posts or videos.

Another Facebook option is to form a private group. Again, this is something you will want to consider when you have more followers. However, a private group where you can interact with your viewers is a popular way to engage your audience. I have a private group for my Etsy sticker and magnet shop that is filled with my best customers. They get first notice of sales and new products, and they can vote on new designs.

You can do the same with your YouTube videos, posting videos in a private group before they go live, answering viewer questions, and holding giveaways. Anything you can do to create "brand" loyalty is always a good idea, and Facebook makes that easy and free!

TWITTER: If you do not already have a Twitter account, you can create one at **Twitter.com.** If you do have an account that you are active on, consider creating a new one just for your YouTube channel.

Note that when Elon Musk purchased Twitter in 2023, he changed the name of the site to **X.** However, most users still refer to it as Twitter.

As with Facebook, you want to keep your personal and business lives separate on Twitter. Make sure your Twitter handle is the same as your YouTube channel. Remember, part of branding is being known as ONE name across ALL social media platforms. You will need a different email address for each Twitter account you create; since you were given a Gmail address when you signed up for a Google account and YouTube channel, you can use that one.

Like Facebook, Twitter provides a free and easy way to connect with viewers and drive traffic to your YouTube videos. YouTube makes sharing your videos to Twitter super easy as there is a Twitter share button under all videos. Simply click on the Twitter icon and link your YouTube account to your Twitter account to share the title of your video and the direct link and thumbnail of your video.

Twitter allows users to share posts of 280 characters or less. While your video's title, the link, and the thumbnail will automatically be put into the Twitter field, you can increase your exposure by adding hashtags. **Hashtags** are simply keywords that follow a pound (#) sign. For instance, when I film a vlog at our local theme park, Lost Island, which is in my hometown of Waterloo, Iowa, I will add some of the following hashtags:

- #lostislandthemepark
- #lostislandwaterpark
- #themepark
- #amusementpark
- #iowa
- #travelvlog
- #vacationvlog
- #visitlostisland

I try to add as many hashtags as I have room for since savvy Twitter users search for tweets using hashtags, which increases the chance of driving traffic to my videos. If I am vlogging at a place that has a Twitter account, I will also tag them in my post.

When you share a YouTube video on Twitter, Twitter automatically tags the official YouTube Twitter account in your tweet. Please do not remove the tag as it is another free and easy way to get more views as people who follow YouTube potentially might see the tag and click to watch your video.

I set aside some time every evening to connect with other Twitter users since I can do this on my iPhone while relaxing in front of the TV. I follow other resellers and YouTube creators, retweet posts I like, reply to posts, and post a Tweet or two of my own. Twitter works best when you actively engage with other users, so spending some time each day networking on Twitter to grow your followers is crucial.

Some Twitter users follow everyone who follows them, which can certainly be a way to build up your followers. You can also "network" with other folks on Twitter by replying to, retweeting, or favoring tweets. As I mentioned, when setting up your Facebook page, you can add all your social media links, including your Twitter URL, in the "About" section of your Facebook business page; hopefully, some of your Facebook followers will also follow you on Twitter. To encourage this, about once a week, post your Twitter link directly to your Facebook page to make it easy for people to click through and "follow" you.

Add your Twitter URL to the list of other links you share on your YouTube channel, both in your channel information section as well as under each video. Remember to add the http:// to your link to make it active so that users can directly click through to your Twitter account.

The **Edit Profile** feature located on your Twitter homepage allows you to customize the look and information people will see when they click on your profile. Add the same photo or logo profile picture that you use for your YouTube, and also use a heading that resembles your channel banner. Write up a brief but fun description of yourself. Put the link to your YouTube channel in the website field so people can click through to your videos. And finally, click on "theme colors" to customize your profile page even further.

Note that Twitter is decreasing in popularity as of late, so don't fret if you aren't initially gaining a lot of followers. Nowadays, most people simply search for hashtags when using Twitter; they may find your post, but they are not as likely as they once were to follow you. However, the main goal is for people to click on and watch your videos. As long as your tweets are accomplishing that, don't worry if your follower numbers aren't increasing.

Personalizing your Twitter profile, posting regularly, using hashtags, and engaging with other users daily will increase people finding your YouTube videos and subscribing to your channel, therefore earning you more AdSense revenue and more sponsorship opportunities. And if you do end up growing a large Twitter following, you will be able to negotiate sponsored content in your feed on that platform.

PINTEREST: Pinterest is often overlooked when it comes to promoting YouTube videos, but, as with Facebook and Twitter, it is another free and easy way to drive traffic to your channel and increase your video views. And always remember that increased video views mean more AdSense dollars!

If you don't already have a Pinterest account, you can create one at **pinterest.com**. If you are already an active Pinterest user, you can just do what I have done and add a "YouTube Videos" board to your account. However, if you have a very diverse Pinterest account with content that is irrelevant to your YouTube videos, you may consider setting up a second account. My content tends to be similar, so it is okay for me to have a "board" for my videos next to boards for my other businesses, including eBay, Etsy, and my books.

Pinterest allows you to create boards where you pin content. You can "pin" content that others have posted, and you can also share your own "pins." Pinterest started as a way for people, mainly women, to "pin" craft ideas and recipes to virtual boards. However, Pinterest is quickly becoming a tool for businesses to get the word out about their products and develop brand loyalty. As you grow your YouTube brand, you will want to make Pinterest a part of your marketing strategy.

As I mentioned, I have a board on Pinterest that I titled "YouTube Videos." As with Facebook and Twitter, YouTube provides a "share" button for Pinterest underneath all videos. After uploading a video to YouTube, I simply click on the Pinterest icon and "pin" it to my "YouTube Videos" board. The video then appears on the feed of those who follow me on Pinterest. They can click through to my video directly from my pin. And if they "repin" the post, then their followers will also see it. I noticed a dramatic increase in traffic to my books and my YouTube channel since I started pinning links to my books and videos on Pinterest.

Just as you should be doing with your Facebook and Twitter links, be sure to link your Pinterest page to your YouTube channel profile and the description bar underneath all your videos. And put the link in your Facebook page's "About" section with your other social media links. Be sure to periodically share your Pinterest link on both Facebook and Twitter to attract new followers.

You may be noticing by now that a big part of social networking is to have all your sites working together. Include all your social media links on Facebook. Post your Twitter and Pinterest links to Facebook. Share your Facebook and Pinterest links on Twitter. Ensure all your sites are drawing traffic to each other, which will help grow your brand and audience. The more you can get your YouTube channel link out there, the easier it will be for people to find your videos and for your channel to grow!

INSTAGRAM: Instagram offers another free, easy, and fun way to interact with your YouTube subscribers and gain more viewers. In fact, in just the past year or so, Instagram has brought my YouTube channel more traffic than Facebook, Twitter, and Pinterest combined. And since Facebook now owns Instagram, you can link your accounts together, getting twice as much exposure with half the work.

To create an Instagram account, go to **Instagram.com.** Again, ensure your Instagram name is the same as your YouTube channel and other social media sites. If you already have a personal Instagram account, consider creating a second one specifically for your YouTube channel and brand as you want to keep your private life private.

Instagram allows you to share photos and "like" and comment on photos shared by others. While you cannot put a full-length YouTube video on Instagram, you can share content and put in links to your channel, both with your photos and in your profile, you can add shorter video clips there, both through **Stories** and through **Reels,** as well as one-minute-long **Posts.**

Instagram Stories: If you are already on Instagram, you likely know that small photos of the people you follow are at the top of the screen. When you click on a person's picture, you will see the "stories" they have posted, both photos and videos. This content remains on Instagram for 24 hours before it disappears. As long as there is a colorful ring around the photo, there is new content to view.

Creating your own Instagram Story is simple. Just tap on the "+" icon on the screen. Where the "+" sign is located, either at the top or bottom of the screen, depends on your phone (iPhone or Android) and which version of the app you are using. Here you can choose to create a regular post, i.e., one that appears in your Instagram feed. Or you can choose **Story, Reels,** or **Live.**

Choosing Story will allow you to upload a photo from your phone's camera roll or a short 15-second clip from your camera roll. Or you can create a photo or video clip right in the Instagram app by using the camera feature. This option is the large round white circle at the bottom of the page. In the same row are the various filters you can apply.

But let's focus on how to promote your YouTube channel in your stories. What I do is post the thumbnail of the video I want people to watch on my channel. I then add the direct link to the video so that viewers can simply tap it on the screen to go straight to my YouTube channel.

But what do you do if you have multiple links? What if you want to provide links to a website, social media accounts, and affiliate advertisers? It is easy, as you use an add-on feature called a "link tree," which allows you to create a page with multiple links that only require one link in your profile to access.

Instagram only allows users to have ONE link in their profile. However, "link trees" enable multiple links. These link trees, or landing pages, are also used on TikTok, which also only allows one link in each bio.

Several companies provide link trees. Most have a basic free option with more advanced paid options. I recommend starting with a free option first, as you can always upgrade later if you feel you need to.

Some link tree/landing page options include:

- **Beacons:** The only option that includes the ability to monetize links.
- **Campsite:** Offers images next to the links for nice visual appeal.
- **ContactInBio:** Considered a close second in popularity to Linktr.ee.
- **Link-in Profile:** Instead of text links, you can add your own

images and make them clickable. The cost is $9.99 per month or $99 a year after a one-month free trial.

- **Linktr.ee:** The first and arguably still the most popular of all the landing page sites. This is the one I use.
- **Lnk.bio:** Minimalist design but limited features in the free version.
- **Milkshake:** Unique in that it turns your "link in bio" into a free website.
- **Shorby:** Features unlimited links and social icons but has no free option. Plans start at $9 per month.
- **TapBio:** Pulls all data from Instagram and YouTube to create clickable "cards."

Once you have your link situation set up and are comfortable using Instagram Stories, it is time to take it up a notch and try Instagram's newest feature: Reels.

Instagram Reels: Reels allow you to create short videos in your feed. The difference between a *reel* and a *story* is that you can save your Reels to your main Instagram feed, making them accessible forever. Remember that a Story disappears after 24 hours. Reels, however, can be permanent.

According to Instagram's instructions, here is how to create a Reel:

"**Select Reels at the bottom of the Instagram camera.** You will see a variety of creative editing tools on the left side of your screen to help create your Reel, including:

- **Audio:** Search for a song from the Instagram music library. You can also use your own original audio by simply recording a Reel with it. When you share a Reel with original audio, your audio will be attributed to you, and if you have a public account, people can create Reels with your audio by selecting

"Use Audio" from your Reel.

- **AR Effects:** Select one of the many effects in our effect gallery, created by Instagram and creators worldwide, to record multiple clips with different effects.
- **Timer and Countdown:** Set the timer to record any of your clips hands-free. Once you press record, you will see a 3-2-1 countdown before recording begins for the amount of time you selected.
- **Align:** Line up objects from your previous clip before recording your next to help create seamless transitions for moments like outfit changes or adding new friends to your Reel.
- **Speed:** Choose to speed up or slow down part of your selected video or audio. This can help you stay on the beat or make slow-motion videos.

Reels can be recorded in a series of clips (one at a time), all at once, or using video uploads from your gallery. Record the first clip by pressing and holding the capture button. As you record, you will see a progress indicator at the top of the screen. Stop recording to end each clip."

Instagram offers the following instructions for sharing Reels:

"With Reels, you can share with your followers, and they can be discovered by the vast, diverse Instagram community on Explore.

If you have a Public Account: *You can share your Reel to a dedicated space in Explore, where it has the chance to be seen and discovered by the wider Instagram community. You can also share your Reel with your followers by posting it to your Feed. When you share Reels featuring certain songs, hashtags, or effects, your Reel may also appear on dedicated pages when someone clicks on that song, hashtag, or effect.*

If you have a Private Account: *Reels follow your privacy settings on Instagram. You can share to Feed so only your followers can see your Reel. People will not be able to use original audio from your Reels, and people cannot share your Reels with others who do not follow you.*

Once your Reel is ready, move to the share screen, where you can save a draft of your Reel, change the cover image, add captions and hashtags, and tag your friends. After you share your Reel, it will live on a separate Reels tab on your profile, where people can find the Reels you have shared. If you also share your Feed, your Reel will appear on your primary profile grid, though you have the option to remove it.

Whether you have a public or private account, you can share your Reel with your Story, close friends, or in a direct message. If you do so, your Reel will behave like a regular Story — it will not be shared to Reels in Explore, will not appear on your profile, and will disappear after 24 hours."

Finally, in addition to your regular Feed, Stories, and Reels, Instagram also offers a **Live** option and the recently added a **Live Room** feature, which allows you to live stream with up to three other people. Here are Instagram's instructions for Live Rooms:

"Instagram Live: *To start a Live Room, swipe left and pick the Live camera option. Then, add a title and tap the Rooms icon to add your guests. You will see people who have requested to go live with you, and you can also search for a guest to add. When you start a Live Room, you will remain at the top of the screen when you add guests.*

As a broadcaster, you can add up to three guests at once or one by one (for example, you could start with two guests, and add a surprise guest as the third participant later). Going live with multiple guests is a great way to increase your reach, as guests' followers can also be notified."

Note that you do not have to do a Live Room; you can go live independently if you prefer. Regardless, the great thing about going live on Instagram is that you can now earn money from these videos.

Instagram Badges are available for viewers to purchase for 99 cents, $1.99, or three for $4.99. Essentially, they function like a "tip jar" for viewers to "tip" creators. Right now, Badges are only available to certain accounts; Instagram will notify you if you are eligible.

The best use of Instagram that I have found is to connect with subscribers on a more personal level. While I talk a lot about business on YouTube and Instagram, I also share select personal photos of my dogs, family, and life. I also post pictures of fun activities such as eating dinner out (Instagram users love food photos!) or attending local events. And I also post funny memes and jokes, which are always a hit and increase engagement.

Whatever my Instagram content, however, the main goal is to further connect with followers who are interested in the content I provide, whether it is on my YouTube channels, on the e-commerce platforms I sell on, or in the books I write.

Just like on Twitter, **hashtags** are a big part of getting your content on Instagram found. I like to include at least three to five hashtags with every photo I share. However, while too many hashtags can clog up a Twitter post, on Instagram, I add as many hashtags as I can think of.

As I mentioned earlier when discussing Twitter, I frequently vlog at the Lost Island Theme Park in my hometown of Waterloo, Iowa. When sharing a Lost Island video on Twitter, I may use a mix of the following hashtags:

- #lostisland
- #visitlostisland

- #lostislandthemepark
- #lostislandwaterpark
- #themepark
- #amusementpark
- #travelvlog
- #vacationvlog
- #rollercoasters
- #darkride
- #iowa

PRO TIP: You can create a long list of hashtags in the **Notes** app on your phone and simply copy and paste them onto all of your Instagram posts. The goal of these hashtags is for the many Instagram users who search for specific hashtags to find yours, so using as many as possible increases your chances of being found. You can also put the hashtags in your Instagram Stories; however, I typically only add a couple because the hashtags take up space on the screen and can distract from the post itself.

Hashtags bring non-followers to my posts all the time. And not all of them end up following me. However, even if they don't follow me on Instagram, they may still check out my profile and click through to my Amazon Author Page or my YouTube channel. And again, driving traffic to the things I am earning money from is my ultimate goal.

When promoting my YouTube channel via Instagram, I post a thumbnail from my most recent video and encourage followers to head over to my channel to watch it. Since the link to my YouTube channel is in my Linktr.ee menu, which is linked in my bio, I usually write something like: "New video now live on my YouTube channel; direct link in my profile @ann_marie_eckhart." The "@" link will take users to my profile page, where the active link to my Linktr.ee menu, and therefore my YouTube channel, will be. Then the user simply clicks on my YouTube channel URL, taking them straight to my channel, where my newest video will be at the top of the page.

As with Twitter and Pinterest, it is a good idea to actively network with others on Instagram by following them back, liking their posts, and leaving comments. I like to spend about 10 minutes a day scrolling through my Instagram feed to check out what others are posting and engage with my favorite posts.

Note, also, that Instagram is an app. While you can see your Instagram feed, edit your profile, and add followers on a computer, you can only add your own posts using the app on your smartphone or tablet. Unlike Facebook and Twitter, which both work about the same on a cell phone or desktop computer, Instagram works best on mobile devices.

TIKTOK: TikTok is the new social media network on the scene, and it has taken off since it launched in 2018. In just a few short years, TikTok has amassed over 100 million users, making it arguably the fastest-growing social media site online.

TikTok is an app-based, short-form video-sharing platform that allows users to create video clips anywhere from 15 seconds to 10 minutes long. Initially, TikTok was used mainly by those sharing music and dance; however, now it is popular with nearly every demographic with a wide range of topics. From cooking and fashion to gossip and vlogging, TikTok now attracts celebrities alongside everyday folks who, even if they do not upload their content, love to scroll through the feed.

TikTok has also gained popularity among businesses that use the site to build their brands and drive traffic to their websites. This includes YouTube creators using the platform to attract views to their videos. You can now switch from a personal TikTok account to a business account.

Just like Instagram, TikTok allows only one link in a creator's profile. If you want to put more links in, you can use one of the "link tree" landing page plug-ins that I laid out earlier. My link is linktr.ee/anneckhart. This one link opens up to show all of my links, including the link to my YouTube channel.

The biggest benefit to a business account is that you can put a link URL link in your profile, which makes it easy to drive traffic to your YouTube channel. While you can put a URL in your profile, it won't be live, meaning users can't click on it.

So how can you use TikTok to drive traffic to your YouTube channel? Any way you want to! It is up to you whether you want to pop on to let your followers know that a new video has gone live or if you want to share a clip of a recent video. Those who successfully utilize the site to grow their businesses post at least once a day on TikTok, so setting up a schedule will help you be consistent.

Just as I do on Instagram, I love to share video clips from Lost Island Theme Park on TikTok. The theme park community is very active on TikTok, so it's not only a fun place to connect with other enthusiasts but it also helps drive traffic to my vlogs. And when people check out my videos, they may also find their way to my Amazon Author Page, eBay store, or Etsy shops. Again, I'm not only earning AdSense on YouTube, but I'm also making money across multiple platforms. And YouTube helps drive traffic to all of my sites.

PRO TIP: A great way to utilize TikTok is to create a post that you can share on Instagram, Facebook, and even YouTube. Here's how I do it:

In my TikTok account, I create a one-minute or less video of whatever it is I want to promote. Let's say it's for a new vlog that I've just filmed at Lost Island Theme Park. I can cut down a clip from the video or I may film a dedicated TikTok video at the park. Regardless, I try to keep the clip under one minute. I added some of the same hashtags I mentioned earlier that relate to theme parks. I may also add text, captions, and/or music. I then publish the TikTok.

Once my TikTok is live, I download the video to my phone. Next, I switch to Instagram and create a Reel with the clip. This is easy to do: I just click on "Reel" and upload the video clip from TikTok that I downloaded to my phone (it will be in my camera roll). After the Reel is live, I share it on my Stories.

I then go to Facebook and post the TikTok to my Facebook page. Note that you can link your Facebook and Instagram accounts to share Reels automatically. Because I have several different Facebook pages for my various businesses, I choose to do this manually so the clip will go to a specific page.

Finally, I upload the TikTok clip to YouTube as a Short. Shorts are for videos that are under 60 seconds, hence why I make sure my TikTok's are under a minute. Using YouTube Studio, I will then copy and paste the text from the description box of a recent full-length video to the description box of the TikTok video. Since I am already in the YouTube Partner Program, YouTube automatically monetizes the Short so I can earn AdSense on it.

In under 10 minutes, I will have created a TikTok, Instagram Reel, Instagram Story, Facebook Reel, and YouTube Short with just ONE video! That's what I mean when I talk about cross-promotion!

YOUTUBE SHORTS: In 2022, YouTube introduced **YouTube Shorts**, which we touched on briefly in the previous section. Shorts let you create, edit, and share short videos. YouTube Shorts are a direct result of TikTok's exploding popularity in the short-form video market. Longer videos are out, and short videos are in. And by short, we're talking 60 seconds or less.

Shorts are meant as a way to engage your subscribers further and also attract new viewers. They are easy to film on your smartphone. You can film clips and piece them together using an app like iMovie the same way you would put together longer clips for a full-length video. Or you can create a Short from your phone right on the YouTube site; here's how:

1. Sign into the YouTube app on your mobile device
2. Tap the plus sign inside of the circle to Create a short
3. To make your Short longer than 15 seconds, tap 15 above the record button to record up to 60 seconds (if you add in music, the video is limited to 15 seconds)
4. Record your clip the same way you would record any video using your mobile device
5. You can undo and redo clips if you wish
6. Tap Done to preview and enhance your video
7. Save as draft
8. Tap NEXT to add details to your video. Add a title (maximum 100 characters) from this screen and choose the video settings. I like to select "private" and finish the Short on my laptop, but you can make it live from your device if you are ready.
9. Tap Select audience and choose Yes, it's made for kids or No, it's not made for kids
10. Tap UPLOAD. If you choose Public, your Short will go live. If you choose Private, your short will remain on Private until you edit it to Public.

Or you can use the TikTok method I talked about earlier and just upload a TikTok that is 60 seconds or less and that doesn't contain licensed music and turn it into a Short. I'm all about efficiency, so if you are already making TikTok's, turning them into YouTube Shorts is a quick and easy way to expand your reach.

YOUTUBE LIVE: Another interesting feature available to YouTube creators is YouTube Live, which enables you to go live on the platform. Whether you go live alone for a casual chat with viewers or host an event with other creators, YouTube Live is another way to engage with followers and attract new viewers.

You can live stream on YouTube with your webcam, mobile device, or encoder streaming. StreamYard is a popular program that makes going live on YouTube easy and with better picture quality than most webcams.

Before you go live, however, be aware of the safety issues that come with live streaming. "Swatting" is a disturbing trend on YouTube where someone will call the police and tell them there is a dangerous situation going on in the location where a live is being filmed. Police will then show up with the SWAT team and sometimes storm the property. If you do go live, be sure to guard your location.

NETWORK WITH FELLOW YOUTUBERS: There is a fine line between networking with other YouTube creators to grow your channel and outright using them to help you. One of the most awkward things I see new YouTubers do is BEGGING people to subscribe to their channel. They stalk successful YouTube channels and leave comments asking the viewers of someone else's channel to subscribe to their channel. Or worse, they send out private messages to the subscribers of other channels asking them to subscribe to theirs.

If you are creating quality content, there is no reason to beg for subscribers. In fact, it is so tacky and frowned upon nowadays that you will likely turn off potential viewers. However, there are ways that you can network with other YouTube creators that are beneficial for both you and them.

First, you want to SUPPORT other channels. Subscribe to the channels you genuinely like, give their videos a thumbs up, leave nice comments, and share their videos via your social networks (I like to share my favorite videos to both Twitter and Pinterest using the "share" buttons located under each video).

Showing your support to other channels not only helps your favorite YouTube creators, but it will likely get you noticed by their subscribers, drawing people to your channel. Again, do these things because you want to support channels you enjoy; you should help other creators without expecting them to return the favor, especially if the channels are much larger than yours.

Suppose you develop a friendly "relationship" with another YouTuber (they are replying to your comments or noticing your Tweets). In that case, it is okay to casually mention that you also make videos similar to theirs. But do so without expecting you will get anything back from them. Let these relationships develop naturally; just like in real life, genuine internet friendships are based on both parties having an equal amount of respect and admiration for one another.

Suppose you find another YouTube creator with the same number of subscribers as you have and who is creating similar content. In that case, you may want to suggest doing a collaboration video with them. Many YouTubers do "collabs" where they partner with another channel to create videos with similar themes.

Video collab ideas include sending each other boxes of goodies to open on camera, answering "tag" questions, or participating in group challenges. If you live in the same area, have gotten to know another creator well, and feel safe meeting them in person, you can even film videos together, posting a video to your respective channels and then directing viewers to go to the other channel to watch the other video. For instance, I have seen several resellers get together to shop at flea markets or antique malls. They each "vlog" their experiences and post them to their channels, encouraging their viewers to check out the other respective vlogs.

Collaboration videos can help you make friends in the YouTube community; everyone benefits by encouraging viewers to check out all the participating channels. People who do collab videos link each other's channels in their video's description boxes, and the videos are then shared via everyone's respective social media accounts.

However, be careful about tying up your business with someone else's. Remember that YouTube is a business, one you are or hopefully will earn an income from. YouTube is littered with friendships that had major fallings-out due to drama. Make sure you get to know another creator before you recommend their channel or collaborate with them.

Create great content, support the channels you enjoy watching, utilize your social media accounts, and let the viewers and subscribers build naturally! After all, you want people to WATCH your videos, not just hit subscribe because they have been paid or guilted into doing so. Subscribers don't earn you AdSense, views do. I'd rather have views over subscribers any day!

YOUTUBE CREATOR AWARDS:

- The **Silver Creator Award is** given to channels when they reach 100K subscribers
- The **Gold Creator Award** is given to channels when they reach 1 million subscribers
- The **Diamond Creator Award** is given to channels when they reach 10 million subscribers

CHAPTER FIFTEEN: BEST YOUTUBE PRACTICES

Great content, good filming techniques, and consistent social media marketing are always enough to gain viewers and subscribers on YouTube. Follow these best practices to ensure your YouTube career is successful and profitable:

Paying For Subscribers: One thing you absolutely do NOT want to do is pay for people to subscribe to your YouTube channel. There are online companies that, for a price, will get people (usually automated computer "robots" or "bots") to subscribe to your channel. However, VIEWS are what create AdSense revenue, not subscribers.

First, people who have been paid to subscribe to a channel will not actually watch the videos. Second, some sites track YouTube channel subscribers, views, and revenue and post the results online, so it is obvious when someone has paid for subscribers, as there will be a sudden massive spike in their numbers. It can actually hurt your channel if you have a large number of subscribers but a low number of video views in comparison.

Other creators can easily see what a YouTube channel has paid for subscribers. So if you are in a competitive category, expect to be called out if you do this. Sometimes slow and steady wins the race on YouTube, which happens when you let your channel grow organically.

Channel Design: When you log into YouTube, you can select **Your Channel** (click on your profile picture in the top left-hand corner and select Your Channel from the drop-down menu) to edit the design of your channel's homepage via the **Customize Channel** icon. Once on the **Channel customization** page, there are three sections you can work on: **Layout, Branding,** and **Basic Info.**

Under the **Layout** tab, you can add a **Channel trailer for people who haven't yet subscribed to your channel.** This acts as a commercial or preview for anyone who comes to your channel but is not yet subscribed. You can also upload a **Featured video for returning subscribers** to give a special welcome back for your loyal viewers. Under **Featured sections**, you can select videos, other channels, or Shorts to group together.

Under the **Branding** tab, you can change your **Profile picture,** which is the photo that appears not just on your channel page but also next to all of your videos and next to any comments you post on your videos or anyone else's.

A **Banner image** appears across the top of your channel. You need to provide an image that measures 2048x1152 pixels and 6MB or less. There are a lot of free apps that can create these specialty images; I use Canva to create my banners, but you can also hire a designer on Fiverr for under $10 to create one for you.

Finally, you can add a **Video watermark** that will appear on your videos in the video player's right-hand corner. An image that measures 150x150 pixels is recommended. The image must be a PNG, GIF (no animations), BMP, or JPEG file that is 1MB or less. My watermark is my YouTube channel logo. You can choose to have the watermark appear at the end of the video, at a specific start time, or throughout the entire video.

Finally, under the **Basic info** tab, you can change your **Name** (the name of your channel) and your **Handle** (a name that will appear with the @ sign in front of it).

Next, you can add a **Description**, which is a great place to introduce yourself to your viewers and explain what your channel is about. Here's mine: *Hi, and welcome to my channel! My name is Ann, and I am an* *author and entrepreneur based in Iowa. On my channel, I share vlogs that include everything from my various businesses (Amazon KDP, YouTube, eBay, and Etsy) to my personal interests, which include my pug dogs and trips to the Lost Island Theme Park in my hometown of Waterloo, Iowa.*

There are fields for the **Channel URL**, which is your unique channel ID. But there is also a **Custom URL** field with an easier-to-remember web address. My Channel URL is youtube.com/channel/UCBRHRiTeLsTpNJGBPYkh4MA, but my Custom URL is youtube.com/c/AnnEckhart.

If you need to change your Custom URL, you can do this by updating your handle at youtube.com/handle.

Next is the **Links** section. Here is where you can add all of your social media and website links. I currently have the following URLs linked: my Amazon store (this is where I have my books and a list of reselling supplies and household favorites), my two Etsy shops, and my eBay store, along with my Facebook, Twitter, Instagram, and TikTok pages.

The last section is **Contact info**, where you can provide your email address. This is meant for businesses and brands to contact you about sponsorships and other opportunities, but don't be surprised if viewers use this email to contact you directly.

Description Box: When you upload a video to YouTube, you need to create a title and put some information in the description box below each video. Your description box should give your viewers directions for what you want them to do, and the first thing should be the most important as it is the only one viewers will initially see unless they expand the view to reveal everything written in the box.

Some YouTubers ask viewers to give their videos a thumbs-up, leave a comment, and subscribe as the first things in their description boxes. Since I am trying to drive traffic to my books, I list my Amazon

Storefront first. Under that, I have all the links to my Etsy and eBay stores plus my social media sites. I also have my disclaimer, which, unless the video is sponsored, reads, *This video is not sponsored. Links may contain referral or affiliate compensation.*

I keep the verbiage in the description box of my videos in a Word document so I can easily copy and paste the information whenever I upload a new video. Because viewers only see the first three lines of the description bar unless they click to expand it, it is vital to put your most crucial directive there. Make sure any websites you link have the complete URL addresses included (https://) so they are "live," meaning viewers can click on them and be taken directly to whatever site you want.

Encouraging Likes, Comments & Subscriptions: While it may seem logical that people who watch and enjoy your videos will give them a "thumbs up," leave comments, and subscribe to your channel, most viewers will not give you any feedback whatsoever. As I mentioned earlier, many people will find your videos through internet searches or YouTube, meaning YouTube is recommending your videos while they are watching another creator's channel. Most viewers do not even have YouTube accounts, so while they can watch videos via the app or on their computers, they cannot respond to your videos in any way.

For viewers with a YouTube account, however, you want to encourage interaction as much as possible. YouTube offers those with a YouTube account the ability to "like" (i.e., click on the little "thumbs up" icon) videos, leave a comment on videos, subscribe to channels, add videos to a "favorites" list, and share videos to their social media accounts.

Encouraging people to do any of the above helps to promote your videos as the friends and followers of those viewers will see their activity and possibly decide to subscribe to your channel, too. I often forget to give the videos I am watching a "thumbs up" and usually only do so when the creator reminds me.

At the end of most of my videos, I will say something like, "If you like this video, please be sure to give it a thumbs up, leave any comments or questions below, and subscribe to my channel for more videos like this!"

Some YouTube creators ask for likes and subscribers at the beginning of their videos, and some even mention it in the middle. What you do is up to you; you can always play around with this to see what feels the most natural.

Monitoring Comments: Having viewers leave comments on your videos is something every YouTuber appreciates...unless those comments are mean. While most comments on my videos are positive, a "hater" comes along and says something rude or nasty now and again.

The more views a video gets, the more likely it is that someone will eventually leave a negative comment on it. The large YouTube channels whose videos get millions of views have to deal with an enormous amount of hate or "trolls," some of it so bad that it has driven successful YouTubers off the site.

Some YouTuber creators do not monitor the comments left on their videos, believing that free speech protects those who leave comments and feeling that any comment, good or bad, is engagement that ultimately benefits their growth. While I am all for free speech, I believe it comes with consequences. The result for someone leaving a negative comment on one of my videos is that I remove the comment and ban the person from my channel so that they cannot interact with me on YouTube in any way, either by giving a video a thumbs down, leaving me a comment, or subscribing to my channel.

I view my YouTube channel as my personal space. I would not allow someone to come into my home and treat me poorly, so I would not let them be mean to me through YouTube. Some creators don't care what types of comments are left on their videos, but I do. Only you can decide what you are comfortable with.

Negative comments hurt, but most people who leave comments are kind and supportive. I try my best to reply to anyone who leaves a comment on any of my videos, although I usually only do this for the first day or two after the video goes live. Even if I cannot leave a written reply, I try to give nice comments a "thumbs up" and click on the little heart icon next to their comment to let them know I saw their comment.

The **YouTube Studio App** makes acknowledging comments easy as you can simply tape the "thumbs up" and "heart" icons. Depending on your mobile device's typing skills, it can be difficult to type out a reply on your phone. But this strategy allows you to quickly acknowledge comments.

You get a notification of activity on your videos whenever you log in. There will be a little red box next to the bell icon at the top of the page with the number of activities – likes, comments, shares, subscriptions – that are new.

I have my **YouTube Studio** bookmarked in my browser so that it is the first page I go to. This takes me to my **Channel dashboard**, where on the left-hand side of the page are several options I can choose from, including **Comments**. Once I click on the comment icon (it looks like a speech bubble), I am brought to a dedicated page where comments are listed in chronological order, allowing me to see the most recent comments that have been left. It is easy for me to reply to or like the comments, delete any that are inappropriate, and check on those marked **Held for review**. I can also select **I haven't responded** to only see the comments I haven't yet replied to.

Often people will continue to leave comments on videos months or even years after they were first put up and responding to those can be nearly impossible unless you go to the dedicated **Comments** page so that you can see the most recent comments that have been left. Do your best to reply to comments, or at least acknowledge that you are reading all comments in your videos.

You want to continually let your audience know that you appreciate all their "likes" and comments. However, the most successful YouTube channels do eventually have to stop reading and replying to comments as it is too time-consuming. At most, I may get 200 comments on a video, but it is usually much less, so it is still manageable for me. It is a great goal to have a video eventually with so many viewers and comments that you cannot keep replying to them!

Privacy: When the internet first became available, people could hide anonymously behind their computers, posting whatever they wanted under screen names without anyone knowing who or where they were. However, social media, and especially YouTube, has changed that. Even if you decide to make videos where you do not appear on screen, you will still expose yourself to the world. Therefore, it is important to take the proper safety and security measures.

Keep the exact location of your home to yourself. I only say that I live in Iowa; I don't disclose the exact city. I don't show the front of my house. I have a P.O. Box for mail, so I don't have to give out my home address. I don't announce if I am going on vacation, not only because I don't want people to know that no one is home but also because they don't show up where I am traveling.

I am a small-time YouTuber, and these measures may seem extreme. However, I am more comfortable with the level of privacy I have cultivated. I would rather be safe than sorry. Once you have exposed the city you live in or shown the front of your house, that information is online forever. Be extra careful when you are filming and even talking so that you do not give away too much of your privacy. Yes, anyone who wants to track you down can if they do enough research, don't make it any easier on them.

Schedule & Consistency: If you want to create YouTube videos to make money and build your brand, you will want to keep a consistent schedule of uploading videos. Some people upload on a specific day of the week, while others aim for a set number of videos per week. I typically like to post on Mondays, Wednesdays, and Fridays. When I had two active channels, I made sure to alternate days so that I was only posting one new video a day across both channels.

No matter what my upload plans are, I try to keep my viewers updated on my schedule. If viewers expect a video, but something has come up, and I cannot upload it, I will try to post an update. I can do this directly on YouTube by posting on the **Community** tab of my channel, which will show up in my subscriber's feed. And I can also post about the schedule change on Facebook, Twitter, and Instagram. Viewers will forgive an interruption in your upload schedule if you keep them informed. And if you can't because of an emergency, they will certainly understand.

Nothing is worse than subscribing to a new YouTube channel that promises frequent videos, only never to see the creators upload again. If you are going to be successful on YouTube, you MUST commit to it. You cannot upload a few videos, abandon your channel, and then wonder why you don't have any subscribers and aren't making any money. Find a filming schedule that works for you and stick to it, at least when you are first starting out.

I recommend starting out with one or two weekly videos and building on that schedule if you want to. The biggest mistake I have seen new creators make is trying to start a daily vlogging channel only to get burned out and abandon their YouTube career altogether. You can always build on your posting schedule, but it is tough to cut back on it as viewers expect videos on specific days and times. Subscribers can become agitated if you take content away without a good reason.

YouTube analytics show that viewers prefer videos that are around 15 minutes in length. Unless you are filming a vlog-style video or doing a live question-and-answer session or hangout, anything longer than 15 minutes is usually too long for most people. However, putting up videos that are too short may not satisfy viewers. And if viewers don't watch your videos, you won't earn any AdSense revenue.

But of course, every situation and viewer is different. I watch channels that put up 10-minute videos and others that produce videos that are over an hour. Again, sticking to your guns and creating the content that pleases you is the most important thing, regardless of video length. Remember that videos must be at least eight minutes long to insert the **Mid-Roll Ad Breaks** we discussed earlier in this book. To maximize your AdSense income, you will want to aim for videos at least eight minutes in length so you can insert those ads.

However, more important than the length of videos is their QUALITY. As we discussed early on in this book, you do not need expensive camera equipment or editing software to produce quality YouTube videos (again, I film and upload videos on an iPhone). Still, you want your videos to be clear, steady, and well-lit. Speak up so viewers can hear you. Be sure you have a nice backdrop while filming a sit-down video. Do your best to provide your viewers with the kind of quality video you enjoy watching.

Before you upload your video and make it live, watch it back first to ensure it looks and sounds nice. I would rather reshoot a video or skip it altogether than upload one that is of poor quality. When I upload my videos, I first have them set to "Private" so I can review them on YouTube before making them public. As my filming has gotten better over the years, I have deleted old videos that were not up to my standards and reshot others when possible.

Views Vs. Subscribers: Most people start on YouTube focused solely on gaining subscribers. And while your number of subscribers is important to your channel's overall growth and your brand, the number of views your videos get is more important.

As I mentioned earlier in this chapter, I have seen people so focused on gaining subscribers that they have PAID people to subscribe to their channels. However, just because someone subscribes to your channel does not mean they will watch your videos. You only earn AdSense revenue from people WATCHING your videos. And brands look not only at your subscriber count but also views when deciding on sponsorships. Paying for subscribers is a huge waste of time and money.

Only when someone watches your monetized videos and sees or clicks on the ads will you earn any Google AdSense revenue. To attract viewers, you need to produce quality content. Not all subscribers will watch all your videos, and not all viewers will become subscribers. Suppose you have one of two videos that draw a lot of viewers from internet searches or YouTube promoting them. In that case, you may make a lot of AdSense money from people just watching your videos, even if they do not end up subscribing.

However, if you are like me and are doing YouTube for both fun and profit, you will consistently need to upload new videos. While I have a handful of videos with current views of over 100,000, as of this writing, most of my videos average about 3,000 views each within the first week, some a bit less and some a bit more. Of course, the longer my videos remain on YouTube, the more views they will get. Your videos will continue to earn AdSense money as long as people continue to watch them. And the more videos you have, the more that money will compound over time.

I focus on creating quality content that I am personally interested in, hoping that the viewers will respond. While I love earning AdSense, I never make a video thinking it will make me money. I make videos that I enjoy filming and hope others will benefit from. Sometimes my favorite videos are the least viewed. However, I just continue making the videos I want to make, and eventually, like-minded people find them.

Making videos is time-consuming, so if I am not having fun, I won't do it. Viewers are smart and will see right through an attempt to film videos strictly done for views. Be yourself, have fun, and the views and subscribers will come!

Dealing With Haters: While most viewers who leave comments on YouTube videos are kind and encouraging, the longer you are on the site, the more likely it is you will encounter haters, also referred to as "trolls," those negative people who hide behind fake names and blank profile photos in order to leave nasty comments.

While it is tempting to fight back against mean commenters, I have found that ignoring them is the best thing to do. These people love to push buttons; they want creators to engage with them in hopes they can escalate the fight. When they realize you aren't going to fight back, they usually leave and find another victim.

What do I do when someone leaves an inappropriate comment on one of my videos? I delete the comment and block the person from my channel. I do the same for anyone who leaves inappropriate comments on my other social media accounts. My stance has always been that if I don't allow someone to speak to me in a certain way in person, I certainly will not allow them to do it online. Especially when I do not even know who they are.

People online can be mean; they lash out because they are unhappy. As the saying goes, "Hurt people hurt people." And since YouTube allows users to hide behind screen names, it is easy for these types of viewers to leave negative comments.

If you are going to be on YouTube, you will have to develop a thick skin. Keep your focus on creating the best content you van and connecting with the viewers who are kind; the bad ones are not worth your time. And, hey, at least they watched your video, and you earned AdSense from it!

CHAPTER SIXTEEN: A DAY IN THE LIFE OF A YOUTUBER

Being a YouTuber, even at a part-time or even hobby level, involves more than just filming and uploading videos. In this chapter, I will share a day in my life of everything I do to film, edit, upload, and release YouTube videos. And remember, I film, edit, and upload everything on my iPhone! Currently, I am using an iPhone 14.

For this chapter, I will be using the example of me vlogging at day at Lost Island Theme Park, which is less than 10 minutes from my house here in Waterloo, Iowa. Lost Island is a $100 million family-owned park that opened in 2022, right next to the hugely successful Lost Island Water Park that was built 20 years prior. It is a highly immersive park that features five distinct realms with a tropical island vibe and an emphasis on the four elements of earth, wind, fire, and water, with a fifth "spirit" land specifically for children.

As a season pass holder, I can go to Lost Island any time I want and I always film when I go, whether it's part of an overall vlog with other footage or a dedicated video of my visit. I use a handheld grip for my iPhone that keeps it steady while I'm vlogging, which is very helpful when walking around outside. Note that vloggers who use digital cameras often use windscreen covers so that the audio doesn't pick up with wind. While there are devices like these for iPhones, I've yet to find one I like.

Vlogging is the easiest way to film. As I walk around the park, I film different clips of the various rides, any food I order, the characters, and the scenery. All of these clips are automatically stored on my camera roll. I don't worry about editing or even deleting footage while I'm in the park. I just keep adding clips throughout my time there.

Note that when I film for a longer period, such as if I'm at Walt Disney World in Orlando, Florida, I rely on a portable charger. This is necessary if you are filming all day long without the opportunity to plug your phone or camera in to recharge or switch out SD cards. However, when I am vlogging in my town, this isn't a problem.

After I have finished filming, I head home. The first thing I do is plug in my phone to recharge and cool down. Then later in the day, I will begin the editing and uploading process.

To start, I sit down with my iPhone and open **Settings**. Under **Display & Brightness**, I click on **Auto-Lock** and change the time to **Never**. Why? I want to make sure my screen does not go into sleep mode, which will stop the video from being saved and uploaded. This is an important step and one that I am embarrassed to admit that I often forget. If the phone goes to sleep during this process, I have to start the upload from the beginning.

Next, I open the **iMovie app.** The app connects to my camera roll, and from here, I can add the video clips I filmed at the park into the app. Clips are arranged chronologically in my camera roll, so I simply add them one after another.

After all of the clips are loaded, I watch the video from beginning to end and make any cuts I feel are necessary. Sometimes this simply involves trimming a clip, other times it means I delete an entire clip.

After I have edited the clips, I save the finished video by clicking **Save Video** within the app iMovie saves the finished video back onto my camera roll.

Once the finished video is saved from iMovie to my camera roll, I **open the YouTube app on my phone** and make sure I am logged into my "Ann Eckhart" channel. Remember that while I am currently only active on one channel, I have two channels. If you end up with two or more channels, the YouTube app makes it easy to alternate back and forth between the two with one click. Once I am logged in, I **click on the + sign inside of the circle** at the bottom of the page to begin the upload process.

I choose the **Upload a video** option, which opens up my camera roll. From here, I select the video I just created in iMovie. I make sure that the **privacy setting is turned to "Private"** so that the video does not go live immediately. Remember that I schedule my videos in advance; plus, I need to do some work on the back end before the video goes live.

I then click **Upload** and wait for the video to be uploaded to my channel. How long this takes depends on the video's length and the speed of your internet or WIFI connection. Hence I turned off the screen saver. I charge my phone while the video uploads as it can be a long process that drains the battery.

Once the video has successfully been uploaded to my YouTube channel, I **switch to my desktop computer** to take care of the back-end details, which is much easier to do on my laptop than on my phone. While you can finish all tasks through the app, it's so much easier to do it on a computer.

On my computer, I log into my YouTube account and go into my **YouTube studio**. I then click on the **Content** icon link on the left-hand side of the page and am taken to my channel videos list. The video I just uploaded should be the first video at the top of the page. I hover my mouse next to the video, revealing several icons. I click on the **pencil icon**, which is called **Details,** to access the **Video details** page.

Once on the video details page, I type in a keyword-loaded **Title** so that people who are not subscribed to my channel might find it. A title is required, although its length is up to you. You have 100 characters available for a title. Sometimes I choose a short attention-grabbing title, but I usually try to add to the title the main points of everything in the video. I also try to make the title sound exciting to encourage people to watch it. There are so many videos on YouTube these days, making it a highly competitive space. You must be creative in getting people to click on your videos, especially when they first go live.

After writing the Title, I go into a Word document I have on my computer to copy and paste a block of text that I put into the **Description** box. Viewers will only see the first three lines of your description box unless they click on it to open it completely. Therefore, you want your most important link to be first. For me, that's the link to sign up for my free newsletter. Then I link my Amazon store, where I have my books, reselling products, and household favorites listed. I also link my Etsy shops, my eBay store, and all of my social media sites.

I also include a **Disclaimer**: *This is not a sponsored video. If disclosed, some products were sent to me for review. Links may contain affiliates/ referrals.*

The disclaimer is important per FTC rules. At the bottom of the page is a **SHOW MORE** area with a **Paid Promotion** section where you check a box to see if you received money for your video or if it includes product placement. If the video I uploaded had been sponsored, I would have also needed to disclose that in the description box and verbally state it in the video.

At the bottom of the description box, I added **three hashtags**, which YouTube will put at the top of the video when it goes live. This is a new YouTube feature, and it works to help people find similar videos through hashtags. For a Lost Island Theme Park vlog, I would likely use the hashtags #lostislandthemepark, #themepark, and #amusementpark. These are the most searched hashtags of viewers looking for theme park videos, so using these tags will hopefully help me reach that audience.

Another area under the **SHOW MORE** section is a **Tags** field. Here, you can add even more words (think of tags as hashtags without the # symbol) to help potential viewers find your videos when they do a YouTube search. I keep an extensive list of these tag words related to my different content, separated by commas, in the same Word document where I have my description box information. I can simply copy and paste this block of words into the tags section of every video. In this case, I would use my theme park list of tags.

As you go alone editing fields on this page, make sure you periodically click on the **SAVE** button to ensure you don't lose your work. I typically click **SAVE** after I complete each field.

Back under the **Description** box is the field for your video's **Thumbnail**, A YouTube thumbnail is the image that appears next to the title of your video. It is the first thing a potential viewer sees, and it is imperative to help get people to click on your video and watch it.

You can use several design apps and programs to create correctly sized YouTube thumbnails. I use Canva, which is available as a free app for both mobile devices as well as desktop computers. YouTube thumbnails need to be 1280x720 pixels; be uploaded in JPG, GIF, or PNG format; and remain under the 2MB limit. Canva has YouTube thumbnail templates that you can use.

To create my thumbnails, I first select an image. Sometimes I will use a photo, other times graphics, and in some cases, I will use both. I typically take a screenshot from my video and use that, to add text within Canva. I then save the finished thumbnail to my computer before going back to YouTube and uploading the picture to my video.

The following section is **Playlists**. Playlists allow you to set up categories for your videos. For instance, I have playlists for Lost Island vlogs, Walt Disney vacation vlogs, eBay videos, Etsy tutorials, and recipes. If you create different types of videos, even if they are under the same general theme, you may want to consider creating playlists.

When someone watches a video in a playlist, it will automatically play the next video in the line-up. Therefore, playlists help keep viewers on your channel and watching your videos. If someone found my channel through an eBay video, they may not want to see theme park vlogs. You can edit your playlists within each video or by clicking on **Playlists** at the top of your **Channel content** page.

The next section is **Audience**. Here you need to tell YouTube whether or not your video is made for kids. According to YouTube, *Regardless of your location, you're legally required to comply with the Children's Online Privacy Protection Act (COPPA) and/or other laws. You're required to tell us whether your videos are made for kids.*

Examples of what may be considered made for kids include:

- Children are the primary audience of the video.
- Children are not the primary audience, but the video is still directed at children because it features actors, characters, activities, games, songs, stories, or other subject matter that reflect an intent to target children.

Examples of what may be considered not made for kids include:

- Content that contains sexual themes, violence, obscene, or other mature themes is not suitable for young audiences.
- Age-restricted videos that aren't appropriate for viewers under 18.

Because my videos are not specifically targeted toward children, I always check the box next to **No, it's not made for kids.**

At the bottom of the **Video details** page is a **SHOW MORE** tab. Here you can access more options, most of which are optional. These choices can seem overwhelming, but they can help your video be better positioned in search results. Options include:

- **Paid promotion:** If you accept anything of value from a third party to make your video, you must let YouTube know. They will then show viewers a message that tells them your video contains paid promotion.
- **Automatic chapters:** Chapters and key moments make your video easier to watch. You can overwrite automatic suggestions by creating your chapters in the video description.
- **Featured places:** Help viewers explore key places in your video. These are public places like restaurants and shops, but YouTube won't display your current location or other private info.
- **Automatic concepts:** Help viewers learn more about unfamiliar terms without leaving the video. Concepts mentioned in your video may automatically appear in the description.
- **Tags:** Tags can be useful if content in your video is commonly misspelled. Otherwise, tags play a minimal role in helping viewers find your video.
- **Language and caption certification:** Select your video's language and, if needed, a caption certification
- **Recording date and location:** Add when and where your video was recorded. Viewers can search for videos by location.
- **License and distribution:** Unless you are using music for which you have the license, allow the default option of **Standard YouTube License** with **Distribution** of

Everywhere.

- **Shorts remixing:** You can let others create Shorts using content from your video. If you don't allow remixing, Shorts remixed from this video will be permanently deleted. I do NOT allow Shorts remixing as I don't want anyone using my content without permission.

- **Category:** Add your video to a category so viewers can find it more easily. Options include *Autos & Vehicles, Comedy, Education, Entertainment, Film & Animation, Gaming, How To & Style, Music, News & Politics, Nonprofits & Activism, People & Blogs, Pets & Animals, Science & Technology, Sports,* and *Travel & Events.*

- **Comments and ratings:** Choose if and how you want to show comments. I choose the option to **Hold potentially inappropriate comments for review**.

- **Giving:** Add a fundraiser to your video.

After you have completed filling out the **Video details** section, make sure to click on the **SAVE** icon before moving on to edit other sections.

Next, I monetize my video by clicking on the **Monetization icon (the "$" symbol)**. Clicking on that dollar icon brings me to the **Video monetization page**. At the top of the page is a **Monetization box**; I select **On** from the drop-down menu. This will allow me to access the option under the **Type of ads** section of the page. I check every box available: **Overlay ads, Sponsored cards, Skippable video ads,** and **Non-skippable video ads.** The **Display ads** option is automatically selected for you by YouTube.

At the bottom of this page is **Location of video ads.** If my video is over 10 minutes long, I can select all three options: **Before video (pre-roll), During video (mid-roll),** and **After video (post-roll).** Under the

During video (mid-roll) option, click on **MANAGE MID-ROLLS**, which brings up a pop-up window titled **$ AD BREAKS**.

Here, I can choose where the ads that run in the middle of my videos will appear. These ads bring in the most AdSense revenue, so it is essential to make sure you place them strategically. Too many ads can turn viewers off, but not enough can negatively affect your AdSense earnings. I generally like to place ads around the six to eight-minute mark of each of my videos, although, for really long videos (over thirty minutes), I will use less so as not to turn off viewers with too many ads.

On the **$ Ad breaks page**, you can click on **+ AD BREAK** to add in however many ads you want to appear. Let us say that the video I am working on is 20 minutes long. I will likely add in two ad breaks. I will then move over to the **PLACE AUTOMATICALLY** column to enter the times of six and twelve minutes, or around thereof. Note that you can also manually place the ads using the scrolling template at the bottom of the page, but I find it easier just to enter the times. Once I am done placing my ads, I click on the **CONTINUE** icon to be taken back to the Video monetization page.

After I have typed in my title, copied, and pasted in my description and tags, and set up my video's monetization, I go back to the main **Video detail page (the pencil icon titled "Details")**. Until now, I have been using the links on the left side of the page to edit my video's information. Now I will focus on the right side of the page and the options that appear there.

I like to schedule my videos, and I do this under the **Visibility** section. When I uploaded my video from my iPhone to YouTube, I ensured it was set to "Private." Now I can change that from **Private to Unlisted, Members Only, Public (set as instant Premiere),** or **Schedule**. I click on the **Schedule** option, which creates a new window of possibilities.

I schedule my video for 2 pm Central time on Sunday, meaning it will stay private until YouTube publishes it at that time.

Note that I could also choose the **Set as Premiere** option so my subscribers would see a live countdown before the video goes live. Premiere also features a live chat option where viewers can chat with one another while the video plays. Some creators schedule premieres to be in the chat once the video goes live to talk with their viewers.

Premieres are a great way to encourage engagement with your viewers by providing you with a way to connect with them directly. Chatting with your viewers when your videos go live does help increase engagement and create more loyal subscribers, so it is something to consider doing, at least occasionally.

Once I have scheduled my video, I click on **DONE,** and the pop-up window collapses. Note that you do not have to schedule your videos to go up at any particular time; you could make them live once you have added your title and description and set up the video's monetization.

However, the YouTube algorithm seems to favor channels where the videos go up on set days at set times. And if you like to film videos ahead of time, scheduling them will help keep you organized. Many YouTube creators will film several videos on the same day and schedule them to go live over the following days or weeks.

Next is **Subtitles.** This section requires you to manually upload or type in subtitles. Large creators often outsource this task to make their videos more accessible.

The next section is the **End Screens**. Here you can add **Elements** to the end of your video that viewers can click on. You can add links to the following: **Video, Playlist, Subscribe, Channel, Link,** and **Merchandise**.

Adding a **Video element** lets you choose from **Most recent upload, Best for viewer,** or **Choose specific video.** I typically select the *Best for viewer option*, but you can decide what is best for each video. For instance, if you referenced another of your videos in your uploaded video, you could select that one.

If you have created **Playlists** on your channel, you can also choose to add one of those to your video. **Subscribe** is another option, and along with **Video, Subscribe** is my favorite option to add. **Channel** allows you to add another channel if you have one. **Link** lets you add a clickable link to a URL that takes the viewer off YouTube and another site.

I typically only choose the **Video** and **Subscribe** elements for my videos; getting viewers to watch another video on my channel and having them subscribe are the two most important things I would like them to do. You want to be careful of loading too many end screen elements as your screen will look too cluttered to viewers, and they likely will not choose any of the options available.

The next box you can open is **Cards,** which, according to YouTube, "are designed to complement videos and enhance the viewer experience with relevant info." Cards help to point viewers to your other videos and off-YouTube content. You have four types of **Cards** to choose from: **Video, Playlist, Channel,** and **Link.**

Video cards allow you to link to another public YouTube video that viewers might be interested in. **Playlist cards** let you connect to another public YouTube playlist. **Channel cards** will enable you to link to a channel you want to direct viewers to; for example, maybe you are doing a collaboration video with another creator, so you create a "Channel card" to link them directly. Finally, **Link cards** allow you to link to **Associate website cards, Crowdfunding cards,** and **Merchandise cards.**

I do not use the **Card** options as I feel like the **End screen** options provide the same benefits. However, as you continue with your YouTube journey, you can take time to play around with the **Card** features to see if they work for you.

Finally, there is a **Products** box that allows you to tag products in your videos and earn a commission from sales through the **Shopping on YouTube** program. This is a new feature from YouTube that, at the time of this publication, was only available for U.S. creators. It offers yet another way to monetize your content. When you tag products in your content, a *View Products label* will show up in the corner of your content. Viewers can select the label to review a list of the products you tagged. Note that you need to apply to this program; even if you are a YouTube Partner, you aren't automatically enrolled.

At that point, my video is complete and ready for YouTube to make it live at the scheduled time!

As I mentioned, I film videos on my iPhone. Here is the step-by-step process I use:

1. I turn my phone horizontally and film clips that are saved to my camera roll
2. I put all the clips together in iMovie and edit out any sections I don't want
3. I save the finished video to my camera roll
4. I make sure to turn the sleep mode off on my phone so that my camera will not switch off during the uploading process
5. I open the YouTube app and click on the upload video + sign that is in a circle icon at the bottom of the page
6. I chose the video from my camera roll
7. I click upload
8. Once the video is uploaded, I switch over to my computer
9. I add in my title, fill out the description box, add in my three

leading hashtags, copy/paste my list of tags, monetize the video, choose a playlist, add my end cards, and finally, schedule the time and date I want the video to go live

Once my videos go live, I share them on my social media accounts. I use the **Share icons** located underneath my videos to post them to my Facebook page, Twitter account, and Pinterest board. I also put up a post on Instagram, both on my page's feed and in my "stories."

And that is it! That is the entire process I go through to film, edit, and upload YouTube videos plus promote them using social media. I am sure that if you have never done it before, it can seem overwhelming. But trust me when I tell you that it will become second nature after you have uploaded a few videos of your own.

The other work I do concerning YouTube is answering emails from companies who reach out with sponsorship or product offers. Of course, driving is often a part of my vlog videos, so I need to track my miles along with any money I spend on my channel. But it is all worth it when my monthly AdSense payout hits my bank account!

I do YouTube for three reasons:

1. It's fun! I like to engage with viewers and have met good friends through the platform.
2. It is great advertising for all of my businesses! My videos help me sell books on Amazon and make sales on eBay and Etsy.
3. I like money! The monthly AdSense deposits go a long way to helping me pay for extras such as vacations or unexpected household bills.

I hope you, too, decide to make videos for FUN and then enjoy the PROFIT!

BONUS: YOUTUBE TAGS

If you watch enough YouTube videos, you will likely or have already come across "tag" videos. "Tags" are simply quizzes or questionnaires that YouTube creators answer on camera. Think back to your school days when you answered quizzes that were printed in magazines, either alone or with a group of your friends. It's the same concept as it was before the internet, except now it's done on camera for anyone to view!

Whether you are looking to start a YouTube channel or already have one, filming "tag" videos is a fun and easy way to create content for your channel and to engage with your audience. You don't need a fancy set up – you simply sit in front of the camera, read off the questions, and answer them honestly. "Tags" are some of the easiest videos to film, so they are a great way to get started on your YouTube journey or to add new videos to your existing channel without having to do the work of thinking up an original topic of your own.

"Tags" have been around since the beginning of YouTube and are extremely popular. So if you are struggling to figure out ideas for videos, then you'll want to give "tags" a try as they provide you with an already proven concept and format. By using the "tags" in this book, which have already been proven to attract viewers, you'll increase your chance of your video being found by people who are watching or searching for "tag" videos.

Some things to remember when going through the "tags" listed in this section:

Order: I have arranged the "tags" in alphabetical order, not in the order of popularity.

History: Note that YouTube started gaining popularity with young girls and women doing makeup-related videos, so many of the "tags" in this book have their origins in the beauty community. They also tend to skew to a younger audience (many tags have school-related questions). However...

Feel Free To Edit: Neither the" tag" questions nor the "tags" themselves are written in stone. Feel free to add questions or omit questions you are uncomfortable answering. If you like the general theme of a "tag" but don't feel the questions really relate to you, change them up. And only do the "tags" that genuinely appeal to you. Viewers want to watch FUN "tag" videos, not videos where the person is bored or struggling to answer the questions. Make sure you look over the questions first before sitting down to film so you are prepared and aren't left stumbling to answer them.

Tag Others: A great way to network on Facebook is to "tag" other YouTubers in your own "tag" videos. After you've finished answering the "tag" questions, end your video by mentioning a couple of other channels where you'd like to see the "tag" done. Let those channel creators know you've tagged them. Even better is to "tag" ALL of your viewers; ending your video by saying, "I now tag all of YOU to do this video and be sure to let me know if you do it!" encourages your viewers to actively engage with you, which creates viewer loyalty and helps to grow your channel.

Best Practices: A general rule of thumb is to put the "tag" questions in the description bar of your video so that others can use your list to answer the questions themselves. If you are doing a "tag" you saw on someone else's channel, be sure to mention them. Not only it is a great way to network with fellow YouTubers, but you also don't want your audience to think you came up with a "tag" on your own when in fact it's been used by many other creators before you.

Create Your Own: As I mentioned, these "tags" are open to editing and revamping. And of course, nothing is stopping you from creating your own unique "tags"! In fact, YouTube could certainly use some fresh, new "tags"; so don't hesitate to make up some new ones of your own!

"Tags" are fun, easy to film, popular, and encourage engagement – add some "tag" videos to your channel and see how they not only boost your content but also drive viewers to your channel!

And now, on to the tags!

THE ACCENT TAG: Different products and activities are called different things in different countries (for instance, we say "sweatshirts" in America, but the British call them "jumpers"). In this tag, figure out the item or action each question is referring to and share what you call it in your country!

1. What is it called when you throw toilet paper at a house?
2. What is the bug that when you touch it, it curls into a ball?
3. What is the bubble carbonated drink called?
4. What do you call gym shoes?
5. What do you say to address a group of people?
6. What do you call the kind of spider (or spider-like creature) that has an oval-shaped body and extremely long legs?
7. What do you call your grandparents?
8. What do you call the wheeled contraption in which you carry groceries at the supermarket?
9. What do you call it when rain falls while the sun is shining?
10. What is the thing you change the TV channel with?

THE AUSTRALIAN TAG: This tag is for the Aussies to answer! If you aren't from Australia but have traveled there, you can certainly alter a few of the questions to relate to your time Down Under!

1. Which state do you live in?

2. What states have you visited around Australia?
3. What do you order at Boost Juice?
4. Golden Gaytimes or Pavlovas?
5. Cricket or AFL?
6. Who is your favorite Australian actor/actress?
7. Describe your formal night in high school.
8. Do you like vegemite? How do you like to eat it?
9. Have you ever seen or petted a kangaroo?
10. Have you ever seen the Sydney Harbour Bridge?
11. Do you say...Mate? G'day? Jumper or sweater?
12. Overall, what do you think of Australia?

THE BABY TAG: If you have a little one, you'll have fun answering these questions! Not only will it make for a great memory to have on film, but it will also help you connect with other parents. Note that you can answer these questions regardless of what age your child is as other moms and dads are always looking for advice.

1. Your baby's weight and height at birth? At 2 months?
2. How many newborn diapers did your baby go through? Size 1's? What brand?
3. How long was your baby in newborn clothes? In 0–3-month clothes?
4. What size diaper bag? What brand?
5. Did your baby use a baby swing?
6. Would you recommend buying a play mat?
7. Would you recommend buying a bouncy seat?
8. Would you recommend buying a bassinet or a pack-n-play
9. Did your child use a soother/pacifier and what brand?
10. One must-have item for your baby?
11. The item you wouldn't have bought.
12. Any advice for breastfeeding or bottle feeding?
13. What works/worked to calm your baby down?

14. What is/was your bedtime routine
15. Your hair and eye color, your partner's, and the baby's?
16. Any last advice for new parents?

BAND MUSIC TAG: This is the first of several music-themed tags in this book. If you love music, these sorts of tags are not only fun to do but they can also help you connect with viewers and other YouTube creators who share your taste in music!

1. Shuffle your playlist and tell us the first 10 songs that show up.
2. How many bands have you seen live?
3. Which was the best band you've seen live?
4. Which was the worst band you've seen live?
5. Have you ever met someone in a band?
6. Have you ever been in a band yourself?
7. Can you play any instruments?
8. Which band would you give anything to see?
9. Do you have any concert tee shirts or other clothing?
10. Favorite song this minute?
11. What's your favorite genre of music?
12. What song has the highest play count in your playlist?
13. What song would you choose to sing karaoke?
14. What song should never be sung publicly unless by a professional?
15. What's your favorite album?
16. What would be the best line-up for a concert festival?
17. Do you subscribe to any music magazines?
18. Kiss, marry, or avoid the first three artists that show up when you shuffle your playlist.
19. Do you have any music posters up in your room?
20. Do you have the same musical tastes as your friends?
21. Have you seen any musicals?

22. If you could see any musical, what would you see?
23. Do you listen to the radio?
24. What's the worst song ever released?
25. Are you listening to any music right now?
26. What was the last song you heard?
27. What's the next concert you are going to?

BEST FRIEND TAG #1: Grab your best buddy and film this video side-by-side. Or, if you both have YouTube channels, you can each film this tag where you answer the questions alone or by interviewing one another and then encourage your viewers to check out your friend's channel for their answers!

1. How and when did you meet?
2. What were your first impressions of each other?
3. What's your favorite memory of something you've done together?
4. Describe each other in one word.
5. What is one thing that annoys you about the other person?
6. What is one thing you each love about the other person?
7. If you could go anywhere in the world together, where would it be?
8. Favorite inside joke?
9. Who takes longer to get ready in the morning?
10. What's the other person's eye color – don't cheat!

BEST FRIEND TAG #2: Here is another version of a best friend tag. This fun video is to be filmed alongside your best friend and can be done in two different ways. One is for each of you to give your own answers to the questions, or you can quiz each other. If you both have YouTube channels, have each of you film a video asking the other one the questions and then cross-promote your videos to draw traffic to both of your channels!

1. Middle name?
2. Mom's maiden name?
3. Favorite sport?
4. Favorite season?
5. Favorite holiday?
6. Favorite film?
7. Favorite ice cream flavor?
8. What 3 things do you (or your friend) always carry with you?
9. What 3 things are always in your (or your friend's) fridge?
10. If you (or your friend) were stranded on a deserted island, what are three things you (or your friend) couldn't live without besides food, water, and loved ones?
11. Favorite 3 songs of all time?
12. Shoe size?
13. If you (or your friend) won a contest and the grand prize was the services of either a cook or housekeeper, which would you (or your friend) choose?
14. Prefer movies or television?
15. Hot chocolate, coffee, or tea?
16. Chocolate or non-chocolate candy?
17. Favorite teacher (or boss if are older and work a job)?
18. Two favorite and two least favorite classmates or co-workers?
19. If you (or your friend) were eating lunch in a restaurant and the food was inedible, would you (or your friend): a. Send it back; b. eat it and not say anything to anyone; c. not eat it and if the server asks, tell the truth; or d. not eat it and if asked, lie and say it was fine.
20. If someone was talking loudly during a movie, would you (or your friend): a. Shush them very loudly; b. move to another section of the theatre, or c. inform the manager?
21. If you (or your friend) won the lottery, what would you (or your friend) buy first?

BOOK TAG: If you love to read, then the Book Tag is for you! There is an active community of readers and book reviewers on YouTube, so doing this tag can help you connect with other book worms out there!

1. Do you have a certain place at home for reading?
2. Do you use a bookmark or a random piece of paper to mark your page?
3. Can you stop reading anytime you want, or do you have to stop at a certain page, chapter, part, etc.?
4. Do you eat or drink while reading?
5. Can you read while listening to music or watching TV?
6. One book at a time or several at once?
7. Do you only read at home or everywhere you go?
8. Do you read out loud or silently in your head?
9. Do you read ahead or skip pages?
10. Do you like breaking the spine or keeping it new?
11. Do you write in books?
12. What is your favorite book of all time?
13. Who is your favorite author of all time?
14. What are you currently reading?

THE BOYFRIEND TAG: This tag is meant to be done on camera with your boyfriend, with you asking him the questions! Note that this is a rather long tag, so you may want to edit out some of the questions or break it into two parts. If you are married, note that there is a "Husband Tag" later on in this book.

1. Where did we meet?

1. Where was our first date?
2. What was your first impression of me?
3. When did you meet my family?
4. Do I have any weird obsessions?

5. How long have we been together?
6. Do we have any traditions?
7. What was our first road trip?
8. What was the first thing you noticed about me?
9. What is my favorite restaurant?
10. What do we argue about the most?
11. Who wears the pants in our relationship?
12. What is my favorite TV show?
13. What is one food that I do not like?
14. What drink do I order when we go out to eat?
15. What shoe size do I wear?
16. What is my favorite kind of sandwich?
17. What is one talent I have?
18. What would I eat every day if I could?
19. What is my favorite cereal?
20. What is my favorite music?
21. What is my favorite sports team?
22. What is my eye color?
23. Who is my best friend?
24. What is something you do that I wish you didn't?
25. Where am I from?
26. What kind of cake would you bake me on my birthday?
27. Do I play any sports?
28. What can I spend hours doing?
29. If I could live anywhere, where would it be?

CHILD-FREE TAG: While it may feel like the only older women on YouTube are all moms, there are plenty of content creators who don't have kids. If you are one of them and are constantly being asked about having children, this is a great tag to do to answer your critics!

1. Do you like or dislike children?
2. Why did you opt out of parenthood?

3. Do you think your childhood experiences and/or parents' actions influenced your decision not to have children?
4. What is the most common reaction/comment you get when people find out you are child-free?
5. Do you have any child-free friends or relatives?
6. Do you think people are aware that parenthood is a choice?
7. How do you feel/react when your loved ones announce they're expecting?
8. Are you worried one day you might regret your decision?
9. For women, don't you want to experience being pregnant?
10. Is your current partner child-free as well?
11. Is it possible to be in a happy, fulfilling relationship without children?
12. Define parenthood in one word.
13. Do you think you would be a good parent?
14. Do you have pets? If so, do you think you're transferring the nurturing and love intended for a child onto your pets?
15. Which child-free stereotype do you not fit?
16. Is it hard to find a child-free partner?
17. Which label do you prefer: child-free or child-less?
18. Do you actively encourage the people around you to think about their reproductive choices?
19. Are you worried about who will take care of you when you're old?
20. What is the best part about being child-free?

THE CHRISTMAS TAG: Do this tag after Thanksgiving or early December as a fun lead-up to the holidays!

1. What's your favorite Christmas movie?
2. What's your favorite Christmas color combination, green and red or silver and gold?
3. Do you like to stay in your pajamas or dress up on Christmas

Day?

4. If you could only buy one person a present this year, who would it be?
5. Do you open your presents on Christmas Eve or Christmas morning?
6. Have you ever built a gingerbread house?
7. What do you like to do during Christmas vacation?
8. Any Christmas wishes?
9. Favorite Christmas smell?
10. Favorite Christmas meal?
11. Favorite Christmas dessert or candy?

THE CLOSET CONFIDENTIAL TAG: If you love clothing, shoes, and accessories, this is the tag for you! This tag is even more fun is you show the pieces you reference, so read over the questions first and pull out the items you want to show your viewers.

1. What is the oldest item is your wardrobe/closet?
2. What is the newest item in your closet?
3. What is the most expensive item in your closet?
4. What is the most affordable/cheapest item in your closet that you use the most?
5. What was your biggest clothing bargain?
6. What clothing item was the biggest waste of money?
7. What are your current 3 favorite clothing items?
8. What is the most outrageous item in your closet right now?
9. What is your favorite piece of clothing that you've gotten as a gift?
10. What is your most comfortable piece of clothing?
11. What is the most uncomfortable clothing item you own but that you love because of how it makes you look?
12. Show us your favorite complete outfit including shoes and accessories.

13. Show us your favorite black and favorite white items.
14. At what store do you buy most of your clothing?

THE DAD TAG: Grab your dad for this sit-down question-and-answer session! Look for the "Mom Tag" later in this book.

1. What was I like as a child?
2. What do you think of my making YouTube videos?
3. What's something funny I did when I was younger?
4. Have you learned anything from my videos?
5. What's a weird habit of mine?
6. If you had to rename me, what would my name be?
7. When we go out to eat, what do I order?
8. What is the one thing you wish I would do?
9. What is something I do that annoys you?
10. What is something I obsess over?
11. Where would you like to see me in 10 years?
12. When were you the proudest of me?
13. What's the worst thing I have ever done?
14. What's your favorite moment of us together?
15. How was I in school?
16. What would you change if you could raise me again?
17. Describe my perfect mate.

DIRTY SECRETS TAG: This tag sounds naughty, but the questions are, for the most part, pretty innocent! If you feel uncomfortable answering any of these questions, then don't hesitate to just leave them out.

1. What was your first cuss word?
2. What was your first R-rated movie?
3. Who was your first kiss?

4. What do you wear to bed?
5. Have you ever caught your parents in the act?
6. Have you ever cheated in a relationship?
7. What kinds of underwear do you wear?
8. Have you ever pooped your pants?
9. Have you ever had a fantasy dream about a celebrity?
10. What is your favorite feature of your crush or significant other?

THE DISNEY TAG: If you love all things Disney, this is the tag for you! Disney fanatics are a big community on YouTube, so this tag is a great way to connect with others who share your love of the Mouse.

1. A scene in any Disney movie you wish you could experience.
2. Have you ever been to any Disney theme parks?
3. When was the first time you went to a Disney Park?
4. An unforgettable experience/moment you've had at Disney Parks?
5. What non-Disney song(s) reminds you of or brings back memories of Disney and/or the Parks?
6. If you could choose any of the characters to be your best friend, who would you choose?
7. Who are your favorite Disney princesses?
8. Name a scene/moment in any Disney movie that never fails to make you cry.
9. What is the first Disney movie you remember seeing?
10. What is your favorite Disney movie?
11. What is your favorite Disney song?
12. Have you even taken a Disney Cruise?

THE DREAM TAG: The Dream Tag is great for both guys and gals of any age, making it one of the most popular tags for all YouTubers to film!

1. Do you dream?
2. What did you dream about last night?
3. How many dreams to you usually remember?
4. Do you have a dream journal?
5. How often do you have nightmares?
6. Do you lucid dream?
7. Do you dream in color?
8. Do you dream in the first person?
9. Do you have recurring dreams?
10. Have you ever had déjà vu after a dream?

THE 80'S TAG: If you were a child, teen, or young adult during the 1980s, this is a really fun tag to film!

1. What was your age range in the 80's?
2. Favorite 80's movie?
3. Favorite 80's cartoon?
4. Favorite 80's TV show?
5. Favorite thing about the '80s?
6. Where were you in 1985?
7. Favorite 80's cereal?
8. Favorite 80's candy?
9. Favorite 80's song?
10. Favorite 80's artist?
11. Favorite 80's fashion trend?
12. Your favorite pastime in the '80s?

8 "HAVE YOU EVER" QUESTIONS TAG: This tag was first introduced as part of a series of tags counting down from 10 to one; I have one through five together in this book as you can easily film one video to cover all five. However, I've divided five to 10 up alphabetically as they have enough questions in each to make up their own videos.

1. Have you ever liked someone who had a girlfriend/boyfriend?
2. Have you ever had your heart broken?
3. Have you ever been out of the country?
4. Have you ever done something outrageously dumb?
5. Have you ever been back-stabbed by a friend?
6. Have you ever had sex on the beach?
7. Have you ever dated someone younger than you?
8. Have you ever read an entire book in one day?

50 RANDOM FACTS ABOUT ME TAG: Film a video stating 50 random facts about yourself! Sounds easy, but most people stumble unless they write out the 50 things beforehand!

50 THINGS NEAR ME TAG: Make sure you are filming in a room with lots of stuff in it so that you can easily grab and show 50 items that are close to where you are sitting! A desk, makeup area, kitchen, or bathroom all work well for this tag as you'll have lots of items within easy reach.

15 QUESTIONS TAG: There are a lot of these numbered, general-themed tags to choose from, making them great for YouTubers of all ages!

1. What do you think you can do well but really can't?
2. What's a difficult word for you to pronounce?
3. What is your favorite TV show from your childhood?
4. What are your virtues and your vices?
5. What's more important: love, fame, power, or money?
6. If you could live in any era/time period, when would it be and why?
7. If you had to redo your entire wardrobe with clothing from only two stores, what would those stores be and why?

8. Can you recall what you were doing a year ago on this day?
9. Do you have recurring dreams?
10. What's your horoscope sign?
11. What does your dream bedroom look like?
12. What position do you sleep in?
13. Who is your favorite vampire of all time?
14. What are you currently wearing on your feet?
15. Do you have neat handwriting? Show us!

GET TO KNOW ME TAG: The "Get To Know Me Tag" is a great video to film for new YouTubers as it offers an easy way for you to introduce yourself to your audience! However, even if you've been making videos for a while, it's still worth doing for your subscribers to get to know you better.

1. What's your name?
2. Any nicknames?
3. When is your birthday?
4. In what city/state/country were you born?
5. What is your zodiac/star sign?
6. What is your natural hair color?
7. How long is your hair?
8. What color are your eyes?
9. What are your best physical features?
10. Ever worn or do you currently wear braces?
11. Do you have any piercings?
12. Do you have any tattoos?
13. Are you right-handed or left-handed?
14. Who was your first best friend?
15. What was the first concert you ever attended?
16. What is your favorite movie?
17. What is your favorite television show?
18. What is your favorite color?

19. What is your favorite song?
20. What is your favorite restaurant?
21. What is your favorite store?
22. What is your favorite book?
23. What is your favorite magazine?
24. What is your current mood?
25. Are you single or taken?
26. Do you have or do you want children?
27. Are you or do you want to be married someday?
28. What is your current career?
29. Do you believe in God?
30. Do you believe in miracles?
31. Do you believe in love at first sight?
32. Do you believe in ghosts and/or aliens?
33. Do you believe in kissing on the first date?
34. Do you believe in yourself?

15 WEIRD QUESTIONS TAG: Most of these questions aren't actually that weird, but this is still a fun and easy tag video to film for all ages!

1. What's a nickname only your family calls you?
2. What's one of your weird habits?
3. Do you have any weird phobias?
4. What's a song you secretly love to blast and belt out when you are alone?
5. What's one of your biggest pet peeves?
6. What's one of your nervous habits?
7. What side of the bed do you sleep on?
8. What was the name of your first stuffed animal, and do you still have it today?
9. What's the drink you always order at Starbucks?
10. What's a beauty rule you preach but never actually practice?

11. Which way do you face in the shower?
12. Do you have any weird skills?
13. What's your favorite comfort food?
14. What's a phrase you always say?
15. What do you wear to bed?

FIVE-TO-ONE TAG: I referenced this tag earlier; it was originally a ten-to-one tag, but the length was ridiculous. YouTube likes videos under 15 minutes, so I broke six through ten down into individual tags but left one through five in a single tag format.

Five "Do"

1. Do you think anyone likes you?
2. Do you ever wish you were someone else?
3. Do you know the muffin man?
4. Does the future scare you?
5. Does your family know you have a YouTube channel?

Four "Why"

1. Why are you best friends with your best friend?
2. Why did you get into YouTube?
3. Why did your parents give you the name you have?
4. Why are you doing this tag?

Three "If"

1. If you could have one superpower, what would it be?
2. If you could go back in time and change one thing, what would it be?
3. If you were stranded on a deserted island and could only bring one thing, what would it be?

Two "Would You Ever"

1. Would you ever get back together with any of your exes if they asked you?
2. Would you ever shave your head to save someone you love?

One Last Question

1. Are you happy with your life now?

40 BEAUTY QUESTIONS TAG: As I mentioned in the introduction to this book, YouTube first became popular with young women making beauty videos. So there are lots of tags such as this one in this book related to makeup, cosmetics, skin care, and hair!

1. How many times do you wash your face daily?
2. What skin type do you have?
3. What is your current facial wash?
4. Do you exfoliate?
5. What brand of skincare is your favorite?
6. What moisturizer do you use?
7. Do you have freckles?
8. Do you use eye cream?
9. Do you or did you have acne-prone skin?
10. Did you ever have to use Proactive?
11. What foundation do you use?
12. What concealer do you use?
13. Do you know your undertone color?
14. What do you think about fake eyelashes?
15. Did you know that you are supposed to change your mascara every three months?
16. What brand of mascara do you use?
17. Sephora, MAC, or Ulta?

18. Do you have a beauty store card (Sephora, Ulta, MAC, The Body Shop)?
19. What makeup tools do you use?
20. Do you use makeup base or primer for your eyes?
21. Do you use makeup base or primer for your face?
22. What is your favorite eye shadow brand and color?
23. Do you use a pencil or liquid eyeliner?
24. How often do you poke your eyes with an eyeliner pencil?
25. Do you use mineral makeup?
26. What is your favorite lipstick?
27. What is your favorite blush to use?
28. Do you buy any makeup on EBay?
29. Do you like drugstore makeup?
30. Do you shop at cosmetic outlet stores?
31. Have you ever considered taking a makeup class?
32. Are you clumsy in putting on makeup?
33. Name a makeup crime that you hate.
34. Do you like colorful or neutral shades of makeup?
35. Which celebrity always has great makeup?
36. If you could leave the house using just one makeup item, what would it be?
37. Could you ever leave the house without any makeup on?
38. In your opinion, what is the best makeup line?
39. What do you think of makeup overall?

THE FUN QUESTIONS TAG: Here's another easy tag video to film that will help your audience get to know you!

1. When is your birthday?
2. What are 3 of your favorite colors?
3. What are your 3 favorite quotes?
4. Are you addicted to YouTube?
5. What are 3 of your favorite shows on TV or YouTube or both?

6. What are 3 qualities you like in a best friend?
7. Do you like your name?
8. If you had the choice to pick your own name, what would it be?
9. What is your fantasy dream?
10. Do you wear makeup?
11. If you could write a book, what would the title be and what would it be about?
12. What makes you cry?
13. What makes you angry?
14. What makes you happy?
15. What is "fangirling"?
16. What are your 3 favorite snacks?
17. What are your 3 favorite foods?
18. What are your 3 favorite drinks?
19. What are 10 random facts about you?
20. What are 3 fun things you like to do?

FURRY FRIEND TAG: If you have a cat, dog, or other pet, here's a tag just for them!

1. What is your pet's name?
2. What kind of pet is it and what breed?
3. How long have you had your furry friend?
4. How did you get your pet?
5. How old is your pet?
6. What are some quirky things about your pet's personality?
7. What does your relationship with your pet mean to you?
8. What are some of your favorite pastimes with your pet?
9. What nicknames do you call your pet?

HAPPY NEW YEAR TAG: This tag video is meant to be filmed close to the New Year; about a week before January 1st is a good time to upload this one!

1. What do you plan to do for New Year's Eve?
2. Do you have any New Year's traditions?
3. Is there anything you love/hate about New Year's family get-togethers?
4. What was your resolution for the past year? Did you complete it?
5. What is your resolution for the upcoming year?
6. What was your favorite thing that happened this past year?
7. What are you most excited about for the coming year?
8. What are three things you'd like to accomplish in the next year?
9. What is your favorite thing to eat for New Year's?

HARRY POTTER TAG: Are you a Harry Potter fan? Then this is one tag you'll want to do!

1. Favorite Harry Potter book?
2. Favorite Harry Potter movie?
3. Least favorite Harry Potter book?
4. Parts of the books/movies that made you cry?
5. If you could hook up with any Harry Potter character, who would it be?
6. Favorite character?
7. What would your Patronus be?
8. If you could have the Resurrection Stone, Invisibility Cloak, or the Elder Wand, which would you choose?
9. What House would you be in?
10. If you could meet any member of the cast, who would it be?
11. Have you played any of the Harry Potter video games?

12. If you were on the Quidditch team, which position would you play?
13. Were you happy with the way the series ended?
14. How much does Harry Potter mean to you?

HOLIDAY TAG #1: There are several holiday and time-of-year tags in this book, many with overlapping questions. However, most have enough differences that your audience won't notice if you do them all (as long as you space them out a bit)!

1. Which holiday or holidays do you celebrate in December?
2. What are you doing for the holidays this year?
3. What's your favorite holiday drink?
4. Candy canes or gingerbread men?
5. What's your favorite holiday song?
6. What's the weirdest holiday gift you've ever received?
7. Have you ever made a snowman?
8. What is your favorite winter fragrance?
9. What is at the top of your wish list this year?
10. What is the most important part of the holidays for you?

HOLIDAY TAG #2: This tag is similar to the last tag, so I'd pick which of the two you like best and simply title it "Holiday Tag", leaving off the number so as not to confuse your audience! Or choose the questions you like best from each to make your own customized tag!

1. What is your favorite holiday movie?
2. Do you like to stay in your PJ's or dress up for the holidays?
3. If you could only buy one person a present this year, who would it be?
4. Have you ever built a gingerbread house?
5. What do you like to do on your holiday break?
6. Favorite holiday smell?

7. Favorite holiday meal or treat?
8. What is your favorite gift you purchased for someone ELSE this year?
9. What is the number one item on your wish list this year?

HUSBAND TAG: Grab your hubby for an on-camera interrogation, err, interview! This tag is meant to be done interview style, not with both people answering the questions. Turn the tables by doing the "Wife Tag", which you'll find later on in this book!

1. Where did we meet?
2. Where was our first date?
3. What was your first impression of me?
4. When did you meet my family?
5. What's one of my weird habits?
6. How long have we been together?
7. Do we have any traditions?
8. What was our first road trip?
9. First thing you noticed about me.
10. What pisses you off the most?
11. Favorite feature about me?
12. 3 things I am good at and 3 things I am not good at?
13. What do we argue about the most?
14. Do I have PMS?
15. Who wears the pants in the relationship?
16. Do I have any weird obsessions?
17. Your nickname for me?
18. What is my favorite restaurant?
19. If I am watching TV, what am I watching?
20. What is one food I do not like?
21. What drink do I order when we go out to eat?
22. What size of shoe do I wear?
23. My favorite sandwich?

24. What is one talent I have?
25. What would I eat every day if I could?
26. My favorite cereal?
27. My favorite kind of music?
28. My favorite sports team.
29. What is my eye color?
30. Who is my best friend?
31. Something you do that I wish you didn't do.
32. Where am I from?
33. What kind of cake would you bake for me on my birthday?
34. Do I play any sports?
35. What can I spend hours doing?

I LOVE FALL TAG: The beauty questions in this tag cause it to appeal mainly to girly girls. However, don't be afraid to omit some of the questions and add in others of your own!

1. Favorite Fall lip product?
2. Favorite Fall nail polish?
3. Favorite Fall Starbucks drink?
4. Favorite Fall candle scent?
5. Favorite Fall fashion accessory?
6. Haunted house, hayride, or corn maze?
7. Favorite Halloween movie?
8. Favorite candy to eat on Halloween?
9. What are you dressing up as for Halloween?
10. What is your favorite thing about Fall?

I LOVE SLEEP TAG: If you love a good nap, this tag is right up your alley! Filming this in your pajamas and in your bedroom will give this video a great ambiance, too!

1. What is your routine before going to sleep?

2. What do you do when you can't sleep?
3. What is your favorite sleeping position?
4. What can I wake you up for?
5. At what time does your alarm clock go off?
6. Snooze or get up instantly?
7. Do you sleep in on the weekends?
8. What kind of weird stuff do you do while you are asleep?
9. How many pillows do you have?
10. What do you wear for bed?
11. Do you sleep with or without socks?
12. What size/how big is your bed?
13. The first thing I do when I wake up in the morning is....?
14. Do you dream every night?
15. What dream or nightmare can you remember?
16. What time do you go to bed?
17. How many times do you wake up during the night?

INSTAGRAM TAG: This tag works best if you have your Instagram page up on your phone or tablet so that you can show the pictures you reference to your viewers. Don't forget to link your Instagram account in your description bar so that your subscribers can follow you there, too!

1. What's your username?
2. When did you create your Instagram account?
3. What is the first picture you posted?
4. How many times do you log in per day and per week?
5. What is your worst picture?
6. Which picture has the most likes?
7. How many followers do you have?
8. How many people are you following?
9. Who is the last person who liked one of your pictures?
10. Name one brand or celebrity you are following.

11. Do any brands or celebrities follow you?
12. Show us your top 3 pictures.
13. What is the last picture on your Instagram feed?

INVADE MY PRIVACY TAG: This tag is filled with lots of personal, relationship-based questions; so be sure you are comfortable answering them all before you start filming! It's also very long, so consider cutting out the questions you don't want to answer and only focus on those you do to save time.

1. Did you wake up cranky?
2. Would you date an 18-year-old at your current age?
3. Do you prefer to be friends with girls or boys?
4. Would you ever smile at a stranger?
5. Can you commit to one person?
6. How do you look right now?
7. What exactly are you wearing right now?
8. How often do you listen to music?
9. Do you wear jeans or sweatpants more?
10. Do you think your life will change dramatically before the end of next year?
11. Are you a social or an antisocial person?
12. If the person you like said they liked someone else, what would you say?
13. Are you good at hiding your feelings?
14. Can you drive a stick shift?
15. Do you care if people talk badly about you?
16. Are you going out of town soon?
17. When was the last time you cried?
18. Have you ever liked someone you didn't expect to?
19. If you could change your eye color, would you?
20. Name something you have to do tomorrow.
21. Name something you dislike about the day you're having.

22. Have you ever liked one of your best friends of the opposite sex?
23. Are you nice to everyone?
24. What are you sitting on right now?
25. Do you think you can last in a relationship for 6 months and not cheat?
26. Have you ever wanted someone you couldn't have?
27. Who was the last person you talked to before you went to bed last night?
28. Do you get a lot of colds?
29. Have your pants ever fallen down in public?
30. Does anyone hate you?
31. Do you have someone of the opposite sex you can tell everything to?
32. Do you like watching scary movies?
33. Are you a jealous person?
34. If you had to delete one year of your life completely, which would it be?
35. Did you have a dream last night?
36. Is there anyone you can tell everything to?
37. Do you think you'll be married in 5 years?
38. Do you think someone has feelings for you?
39. Do you think someone is thinking about you right now?
40. Did you have a good day yesterday?
41. Were you in a relationship two months ago?
42. Is your life anything like it was two years ago?
43. If the person you wish to be with were with you, what would you be doing right now?
44. What is (or was) the best part of school?
45. Do you (or did you) pass notes in school?
46. Do you replay things that have happened over and over in your head?

47. Were you single last summer?
48. What are you supposed to be doing right now?
49. Don't tell me lies: Is the last person you texted attractive?

LYRICS TAG: Answer all of the following questions with lyrics from songs performed by ONE band or artist. For instance, only answer with lyrics from Elvis songs, i.e. you could answer the question "Tell us the story of your life" with "I ain't nothin' but a hound dog!" This is a tough tag and one you'll want to figure out the answers to before you start filming. If you are finding it too hard, then try answering the questions with any song lyrics, not sticking to a single artist.

1. Describe how you feel today.
2. Describe your best friend.
3. How many times have you been rejected?
4. Tell us the story of your life.
5. How do you act when you are around somebody you like?
6. What did you do today?
7. What has been the craziest thing you have ever done?
8. Describe your favorite concert.
9. Describe how you react when you hear your favorite song on the radio.
10. How many siblings do you have?
11. Complete the sentence: "I am addicted to..."
12. Complete the sentence: "My favorite singer makes me..."
13. How many people have you kissed in your life?
14. How do you feel about drugs?
15. Complete the sentence: "I constantly..."
16. Complete the sentence: "I am..."
17. When people wake you up in the middle of the night, what do you do?
18. Describe your favorite movie.

THE MINI BOYFRIEND TAG: This isn't a tag for tiny boyfriends; it's just a shorter version of the main "Boyfriend Tag"! Do this tag interview style, with you asking your boyfriend the questions.

1. Where did we meet?
2. What was our first date?
3. Where was our first kiss and how was it?
4. When did you know I was the one for you?
5. What was your first impression of me?
6. When did you meet my family?
7. Do we have any traditions as a couple?
8. What was our first road trip together?
9. Who said "I love you" first and where were we at?
10. What do we argue about the most?
11. Do you know any of each other's exes?
12. What is your job?
13. Who wears the pants in our relationship?

THE MOM TAG: This is similar to the "Dad Tag" that appeared earlier in this book, except for this one you are to interview your mom on camera!

1. What was I like as a child?
2. What do you think of my making YouTube videos?
3. What's something funny I did when I was younger?
4. Have you learned anything from me in relation to the content I create for YouTube?
5. What's a weird habit of mine?
6. If you had to rename me, what would my name be?
7. When we go out to eat, what do I order?
8. What is the one thing you wish I would do?
9. What is something I do that annoys you?
10. What is something I obsess over?

11.   Where would you like to see me in 10 years?
12.   When were you the proudest of me?
13.   What's the worst thing I have ever done?
14.   What's your favorite moment of us together?
15.   How was I in school?
16.   What would you change if you could raise me again?
17.   Describe my perfect mate.

MUSIC TAG #1: I think there are just as many music-related tags as there are beauty-themed ones! Here's yet another one where you can share your love of music with your viewers.

1.   Favorite music genre?
2.   Favorite album you own a hard copy of (not digital)?
3.   Do you subscribe to any music magazines?
4.   Do you own any concert clothing?
5.   What is your dream concert to attend?
6.   What is your guilty pleasure song?
7.   From what artist do you own the most albums?
8.   In your digital playlist, from what artist do you have the most songs downloaded?
9.   Last song you listened to?
10.   How many songs do you have on your phone/MP3 player?
11.   Your favorite solo artist?
12.   Your favorite band?
13.   Least favorite musical genre?
14.   First song you ever downloaded.
15.   Can you plan any instruments?
16.   One artist you want to meet in person.
17.   An old artist or band you would like to see make a comeback.
18.   What are your top 5 favorite albums you own?
19.   What is your all-time favorite music video?

MUSIC TAG #2: Yup, another music tag! As you will see in this tag and other similar ones, often the questions repeat themselves. It's good to choose only one tag to film (or if you do all of them, space them out a bit), or pull the best questions from each of them to create your own unique version!

1. Favorite band/musician of the moment?
2. One band you always come back to?
3. Favorite movie soundtrack?
4. What is/are your favorite song(s) of all time?
5. Most embarrassing song on your iTunes?
6. Top 3 played songs on your iTunes?
7. Favorite concert you've attended?
8. Most underrated musician in your opinion?
9. Favorite quote or song lyric?

MUST TAG #3: While this is yet another music tag, it does have more original questions than the others in this book!

1. The Beatles or The Stones?
2. Pink Floyd or Led Zeppelin?
3. First album you ever bought.
4. Favorite album of all time?
5. Do you play any instruments? In your mind, when playing your instrument, do you pretend to be anyone?
6. On a scale of 1-10, how cool do you think Iggy Pop is, or was?
7. If you had to be a groupie/roadie of any band, who would it be?
8. When did you last air guitar?
9. When did you last dance on your own like an idiot?
10. On a scale of 1-10, how good of a dancer are you?
11. Best concert you've ever been to?

12. Do you share any musical tastes with your parents?
13. What are your three favorite genres of music?
14. Which decade do you wish you'd grown up in so you could have lived through that generation of music?
15. Favorite guilty pleasure music?
16. If you had to choose to only listen to one song forever, what would it be?
17. Do you write music?
18. Do you still buy CDs/albums or do you download your music?
19. Favorite guitar solo?
20. Which song would you karaoke to?

MY FIRST TIME TAG #1: The "first time" tags are much more innocent than they sound, although their suggestive titles do tend to bring in more viewers!

1. First Tweet?
2. First YouTube video?
3. First-person you subscribed to on YouTube?
4. First Facebook profile pic?
5. Do you still talk to your first love?
6. What was your first alcoholic drink?
7. What was your first job?
8. What was your first car?
9. Who was the first person to text you today?
10. Who is the first person you thought of this morning?
11. Who was your first-grade teacher?
12. Where did you go on your first ride on an airplane?
13. Who was your first best friend and do you still talk?
14. Where was your first sleepover?
15. What was the first thing you did this morning?
16. What was the first concert you ever went to?

17. First broken bone?
18. First piercing?
19. First foreign country you've gone to?
20. First movie you remember seeing.
21. When was your first detention?
22. Who was your first roommate?
23. If you had one wish, what would it be?
24. What was the first sport you were involved in?
25. What is the first thing you do when you get home?
26. When was your first kiss?

MY FIRST TIME TAG #2: This tag has a lot of the same questions as the last one; again, I recommend you choose only one to do or combine your favorite questions from each into one video!

1. First YouTube video you ever watched?
2. First person you subscribed to on YouTube.
3. Do you still talk to your first love?
4. First kiss?
5. First alcoholic drink?
6. First car?
7. First job?
8. First pet?
9. First celebrity crush?
10. First real boyfriend/girlfriend?
11. Who was the first person to text you today?
12. Who was your first-grade teacher?
13. Where was your first sleepover?
14. What was the first thing you did this morning?
15. First concert you ever went to?
16. First broken bone?
17. First movie you remember seeing.
18. First sport you were involved in.

19. First tweet?
20. First Facebook profile pic?
21. First piercing?

THE 90'S TAG: If you were a child, teen, or young adult in the 1990s, this is a fun tag that will take you back in time!

1. Favorite Disney Channel original movie?
2. Favorite music artist?
3. Favorite Nick Jr. show?
4. Favorite candy as a kid?
5. Favorite game you played as a kid?
6. Favorite McDonald's Happy Meal toy?
7. Favorite book?
8. Favorite clothing store?
9. What would you watch when you got home from school?
10. Favorite TV show?
11. Favorite toys?
12. Favorite commercials?
13. NSYNC or Backstreet Boys?
14. Weirdest fashion trend?
15. Favorite collectible?
16. Favorite Beanie Baby?
17. How many Tamagotchis did you go through?
18. Favorite gaming system and video game?

19 QUESITONS TAG: This is a fun, and easy, "get to know me" tag to film for your audience!

1. Where were you born?
2. Were you named after someone?
3. When was the last time you cried?
4. Do you have any kids?

5. If you were another person, would you be friends with you?
6. Do you have any pets?
7. Do you use sarcasm?
8. Would you bungee jump?
9. What is your favorite cereal?
10. What is your eye color?
11. Do you like sad or happy endings in movies?
12. Do you have any brothers or sisters?
13. Do you prefer the computer or television?
14. What is the first thing you notice about a person?
15. What is your favorite smell?
16. What's the furthest you've ever been from home?
17. Do you have any special talents?
18. Do you have any hobbies?
19. Are you currently in love?

9 "WHAT" TAG: This is one of the tags I talked about earlier in this book as originally being part of a 6-10 tag. However, I have broken them up into their own tags as each is long enough to dedicate a single video to.

1. Your mother's name?
2. What did you do last weekend?
3. What is the most important part of your life?
4. What would you rather be doing right now?
5. What did you last cry over?
6. What always makes you feel better when you're upset?
7. What's the most important thing you look for in a significant other?
8. What are you worried about?
9. What did you have for breakfast?

100 QUESTIONS TAG: This is definitely the longest tag currently being done on YouTube! To keep your video under 20 minutes, try to keep your answers to "yes", "no" or just a few words.

1. Do you sleep with your closet doors open or closed?
2. Do you take shampoos and conditioner bottles from hotels?
3. Do you sleep with the sheets tucked in or out?
4. Have you ever stolen a street sign?
5. Do you like to use Post-It notes?
6. Do you cut out coupons but never use them?
7. Would you rather be attacked by a big bear or a swarm of bees?
8. Do you have freckles?
9. Do you always smile for pictures?
10. What is your biggest pet peeve?
11. Do you ever count your steps when you walk?
12. Have you ever peed in the woods?
13. Have you ever pooped in the woods?
14. Do you ever dance even if there is no music playing?
15. Do you chew your pens and pencils?
16. How many people have you slept with this week?
17. What size is your bed?
18. What is your favorite song this week?
19. Is it okay for guys to wear pink?
20. Do you still watch cartoons?
21. What is your least favorite movie?
22. Where would you bury hidden treasure if you had some?
23. What do you drink with dinner?
24. What do you dip a chicken nugget in?
25. What is your favorite food?
26. What movie could you watch over and over again?
27. Last person you kissed?

28. Were you ever a boy/girl scout?
29. Would you ever strip or pose nude in a magazine?
30. When was the last time you wrote a letter to someone on paper?
31. Can you change the oil on a car?
32. Ever gotten a speeding ticket?
33. Ever run out of gas?
34. Favorite kind of sandwich?
35. Best thing to eat for breakfast?
36. What is your usual bedtime?
37. Are you lazy?
38. When you were a kid, what did you dress up as on Halloween?
39. What is your astrological sign?
40. How many languages can you speak?
41. Do you have any magazine subscriptions?
42. Which are better, Legos or Lincoln Logs?
43. Are you stubborn?
44. Who was better, Leno or Letterman?
45. Ever watch soap operas?
46. Are you afraid of heights?
47. Do you sing in the car?
48. Do you sing in the shower?
49. Do you dance in the car?
50. Ever used a gun?
51. Last time you got a portrait taken by a photographer?
52. Do you think musicals are cheesy?
53. Is Christmas stressful?
54. Ever eaten a pierogi?
55. Favorite type of fruit pie?
56. Occupations you wanted to be when you were a kid?
57. Do you believe in ghosts?

58. Ever have a Déjà-vu feeling?
59. Take a daily vitamin?
60. Wear slippers?
61. Wear a bathrobe?
62. What do you wear to bed?
63. First concert?
64. Walmart, Target, or Kmart?
65. Nike or Adidas?
66. Cheetos or Fritos?
67. Peanuts or sunflower seeds?
68. Ever heard of the group Tres Bien?
69. Ever taken dance lessons?
70. Is there a profession you picture your future spouse doing?
71. Can you curl your tongue?
72. Ever won a spelling bee?
73. Have you ever cried because you were so happy?
74. Own any record albums?
75. Own a record player?
76. Regularly burn incense?
77. Ever been in love?
78. Who would you like to see in concert?
79. What was the last concert you saw?
80. Hot or cold tea?
81. Tea or coffee?
82. Sugar or Snickerdoodle cookies?
83. Can you swim?
84. Can you hold your breath without holding your nose?
85. Are you patient?
86. DJ or band at a wedding?
87. Ever won a contest?
88. Have you had any plastic surgery?
89. Which are better, black or green olives?

90. Can you knit or crochet?
91. Best room for a fireplace?
92. Do you want to get married?
93. If you are married already, how long have you been married?
94. Who was your high school crush?
95. Do you cry and throw a fit until you get your own way?
96. Do you have kids?
97. Do you want kids or more kids?
98. What's your favorite color?
99. What is something memorable that happened to you in middle school?
100. Do you miss anyone right now?

ROOMMATE TAG: This is a great tag for college students to film together! If you are out of school, you can still film it if your former roommate lives nearby or is visiting!

1. Did you guys know each other before you became roommates?
2. What did you guys initially think of each other the first time you met?
3. How long did it take until you guys became friends?
4. What do you guys usually argue about?
5. What is one thing that really bothers you that your roommate does?
6. Do you guys both have the same passion for makeup?
7. What does your roommate think of you making YouTube videos?
8. Who spends the most time getting ready in the morning?
9. What was something that you two didn't notice about each other until you became roommates?
10. Do you guys sometimes get fed up with each other from seeing each other too often?

11. How do you avoid tension while living together?
12. What's one rule you guys have while living together?
13. How do you deal with sharing a bathroom?
14. Do you make two separate dinners at night?
15. Nationalities?
16. Do you use your roommate's things without asking?
17. What are your favorite things that you like to do with each other?
18. What happens when one person gets sick?
19. Have you thought about having pets or a pet?
20. What is the funniest thing you've ever done together?
21. Has being roommates helped or hurt your friendship?

17 RANDOM QUESTIONS TAG: This is yet another easy-to-film, get-to-know-you tag, although this one does have some original questions that you won't find in other tags!

1. How did you get your YouTube username?
2. If you could change your first name to anything, what would it be and why?
3. If you could go back in time and give your younger self advice, what would it be?
4. How old were you when you first learned to blow a bubblegum bubble?
5. What did you want to be when you were little?
6. What do you order at Starbucks?
7. What's the hardest you ever laughed?
8. If you could play any musical instrument, what would it be and why?
9. What's your favorite thing to do when you are upset?
10. What's your favorite movie?
11. What's one food you cannot live without?
12. What's your favorite dessert?

13. What's your favorite pizza topping?
14. Would you rather have the superpower to read minds or the power to be invisible?
15. What did you do for your last birthday?
16. If you had one personal "selfish" wish, what would it be and why?
17. If you were a Pokemon, what would you be called and what would you look like?

THE SCARY TAG: Love horror movies and haunted houses? Then this tag is just for you!

1. What is the scariest experience you've had to date?
2. Have you ever had a scary paranormal experience?
3. Do you know anyone who has been convicted of a violent crime?
4. Do you like scary movies? If so, what is your favorite?
5. Do you like visiting haunted houses for Halloween?
6. Are you afraid of the dark?
7. Does your town have any scary legends?
8. What is your favorite urban legend?
9. Do you frequently have nightmares?
10. What is the scariest nightmare you've ever had?

THE SEVEN DEADLY SINS OF BEAUTY TAG: As I've mentioned several times, the beauty community was one of the first to become popular on YouTube. This is one of the first beauty-related tags to pop up, which means nearly every beauty lover on YouTube has filmed it!

1. GREED: What is your most inexpensive beauty item? What is your most expensive?
2. WRATH: What beauty products do you have a love/hate

relationship with?

3. GLUTTONY: What are your most delicious beauty products?
4. SLOTH: What beauty product do you neglect due to laziness?
5. PRIDE: What beauty product gives you the most self-confidence?
6. LUST: What physical attributes do you find most attractive in the opposite sex?
7. ENVY: What beauty/clothing/accessory items would you most like to receive as a gift?

THE SEVEN "WHO" TAG: Here we are at another of the 6-10 tags I've referenced several times already. This tag of seven questions all focus on the people in your life!

1. Who was the last person you saw?
2. Who was the last person you texted?
3. Who was the last person you hung out with?
4. What was the last person to call you?
5. Who did you last hug?
6. Who is the last person who texted you?
7. What was the last person you said "I love you" to?

THE SHOPAHOLIC TAG: Love to shop? Then grab your camera to film this tag and connect with your fellow shopaholics!

1. Would you consider yourself a shopaholic?
2. How would you classify your style?
3. What store can you not leave without buying at least one thing?
4. Where do you find the best deals?
5. What designer are you willing to splurge on?

6. Do you have a "go-to" shopping outfit?
7. What is your guilty clothing pleasure?
8. What is one staple clothing piece you cannot live without?
9. What is a trend you hope never goes out of style?
10. What trend did you love that passed way too quickly?
11. Who is your fashion icon?

THE SISTER TAG: This is a fun tag just for sisters! If both of you have a YouTube channel, consider filming two versions of this with you interviewing each other in separate videos. Upload one to each of your channels and then cross-promote them. When doing cross-promotional videos, make sure to release both videos at the same time and to mention AND include the links to the other channel in your description bar.

1. How old are both of you?
2. Describe each other in one word.
3. Do people ever get you mixed up?
4. What is something that annoys you about one another?
5. What is it like being sisters with a YouTuber?
6. Do you ever argue?
7. What's the best thing about one another?
8. Dish the dirt on each other!
9. Favorite inside joke?
10. Favorite memory together?
11. Are you full, half, or stepsisters?
12. Guess each other's favorite singer/band?
13. Who takes longer to get ready?
14. Heels or flats?
15. Pants or dresses?
16. Favorite animal?
17. If your house was burning down and your entire family and pets were sure to be okay, what one item would you save and

why?

18. Comedy, horror, or chick-flick movies?
19. Android or iPhone?
20. Favorite movie?
21. What is something weird that you each eat?
22. Do you have any matching clothing?
23. What is each of your favorite TV shoes?

SMALL YOUTUBER TAG: Have you just started making YouTube videos? Do you dream of one day having millions of subscribers but feel like you aren't growing fast enough? Don't worry, you aren't alone as there are many other small YouTubers out there. This tag not only helps your viewers get to know you, but it can also help you connect with other start-up YouTube channels, which can lead to shout-outs and collaborations!

1. What inspired you to start making videos?
2. How long have you been on YouTube, and have you had other channels in the past?
3. Where do you see yourself and your YouTube channel in 5 years?
4. What message are you trying to get across with your videos?
5. Have your friends and family found your channel?
6. What does your username mean?
7. Who is your favorite YouTuber?

6 "WHERE" TAG: Here we are back to that 6-10 tag that I broke up into individual videos. This one features all location-based questions and is super quick to film!

1. Where does your best friend live?
2. Where did you last go?
3. Where did you last hang out?

4. Where do you or did you go to school?
5. Where is your favorite place to be?
6. Where did you sleep last night?

THE TAN LINES TAG: This tag should be called the "summer tag", but for some reason, it goes by the name "tan lines tag". Regardless of the title, if you love being outside in the warm weather, you'll have fun filming this video!

1. A house on the beach or a house near the lake?
2. Favorite summer hairstyle?
3. Do you get easily tanned or do you get easily burned?
4. Have you ever got a henna tattoo done?
5. Campfire or late-night swimming?
6. If you could go somewhere during summer where would you go?
7. Bikinis or swimsuits?
8. Summer make-up must-have?
9. How many degrees was it on the hottest day until now where you are at?
10. Have you ever had a summer love?
11. Number one thing on your summer bucket list?
12. Long or short hair during summer?
13. Do you wear make-up if you're going to the pool or beach?
14. Worst summer memory?

TEENAGE GIRL TAG: This tag was originally entitled the "Common White Girl Tag", but I found that so offensive that I changed the title specifically for this book. ALL girls, regardless of skin color, can have fun filming this video!

1. Favorite Starbucks drink?
2. How long does it take you to get ready in the morning?

3. How many selfies do you take daily?
4. How many Instagram followers do you have?
5. Do you ever say "LOL" or "OMG" out loud?
6. Do you wear the same clothing item more than once without washing it?
7. How many Tweets do you have?
8. Instagram, Twitter, or Tumblr?
9. What do you spend most of your time doing?
10. Who are your favorite YouTubers?
11. How often do you do your nails?
12. Are you a shopaholic?
13. How many times have you watched "Mean Girls"?
14. Do you own a lot of clothes?
15. Do you take pictures of your food before eating to share on social media?
16. Do you wear make-up every day?
17. What are your average grades in school?
18. How do you usually style your hair?
19. Do you always look presentable?

10 "HOW" TAG: Here's number ten of the 6-10 tags that I broke up into individual videos. This tag focuses solely on "how" questions!

1. How did you get one of your scars?
2. How did you celebrate your last birthday?
3. How are you feeling at this moment?
4. How did your night go last night?
5. How did you do in high school?
6. How did you get the shirt you're wearing?
7. How often do you see your best friend(s)?
8. How much money did you spend on frivolous things last month?
9. How old do you want to be when you get married (or how

old would you be if you were already married)?

10. How old will you be at your next birthday?

10 LITTLE BEAUTY SECRETS TAG: Another beauty tag – shocker! This one is short and sweet and does contain some unique questions that differ from the other beauty videos.

1. What is the one product that makes you feel like a million dollars?
2. What is your skincare secret?
3. What is your hair care secret?
4. Any workout tips?
5. Which perfume is your secret weapon?
6. Show a clothing item of yours that always turns heads.
7. What is your most treasured piece of jewelry?
8. Who is your style crush?
9. Tell us something about you that we don't know!

10 UNDERRATED YOUTUBE GURUS TAG: If you spend lots of time watching YouTube videos, this is a great tag to film as it helps you spread the word about your favorite creators and connect with other viewers who enjoy those channels, too!

1. First person that came to mind when you heard the name of the tag?
2. Someone on YouTube that reminds you of yourself?
3. Someone you watch for pure entertainment.
4. Someone with incredible style?
5. Someone with flawless makeup?
6. Someone with perfect hair?
7. Someone with fewer subscribers than you?
8. Someone with more subscribers than you?
9. Someone whose channel you just found.

10. The person with the most potential to grow?

THANKSGIVING TAG: Even though Thanksgiving is an American holiday, lots of people around the world are starting to incorporate it into their Novembers!

1. What is your favorite Thanksgiving side dish?
2. What is your favorite Thanksgiving dessert?
3. Do you like just the turkey, just the side dishes, or both?
4. What does your ideal Thanksgiving outfit look like?
5. What is your best Thanksgiving memory?
6. How many words can you make of the word "GOBBLE"?
7. Least favorite Thanksgiving dish?
8. Do you have any quirky Thanksgiving family traditions?
9. Where do you and your family usually celebrate Thanksgiving?
10. What are you most thankful for?

30 QUESTIONS MUSIC TAG: I told you that beauty and music tags were the most popular, and here we are at another musically focused video! At 30 questions, this one is long, so keep your answers short to ensure your video doesn't go on for ages (ideally, you want to keep all videos around 15 minutes).

1. The last song you listened to?
2. Last song you purchased?
3. Song you discovered on YouTube.
4. Favorite soundtrack piece?
5. Favorite band?
6. Favorite solo artist?
7. Favorite album?
8. Best live gig or act you want to see live?
9. Guilty pleasure song?

10. Song you used to hate but now you like.
11. Song you used to love but now can't stand.
12. Group you wish had never split.
13. Favorite song from a video game?
14. Favorite song from a film?
15. Favorite song from a commercial?
16. Song you grew up with.
17. First song/alum you ever bought?
18. Album you found accidentally and love.
19. Favorite foreign language song?
20. A song from the year you were born.
21. Song from your favorite music genre?
22. Most overrated song?
23. Song you would recommend to everyone.
24. Song that reminds you of a specific event?
25. Song you can't help but sing along to?
26. Favorite parody song?
27. Favorite slow song?
28. Favorite fast song?
29. Favorite song at the moment?
30. All-time favorite song

THE THROWBACK TAG: This nostalgic tag is fun for all ages to film!

1. What year were you born?
2. Do you have pictures of yourself from when you were younger? If some, show a few on camera.
3. What television shows did you watch growing up?
4. What did you want to be when you grew up; and have you become that, or do you still want to be that?
5. What were your favorite toys to play with as a child?
6. What's your most embarrassing childhood memory?

7. What music did you love to listen to as a child?
8. What were some of the Halloween costumes you wore as a kid?
9. Do you have any special mementos you've kept since childhood?
10. Did you have any weird habits as a child?
11. What's the scariest thing you remember that happened to you as a child?
12. How is the world different now from the way it was when you were growing up?

13 QUESTIONS TAG: Here is another get-to-know-you tag. None of these questions are very serious, so even the most private or shy YouTube creators should have no problem filming this video!

1. What do you order at Starbucks?
2. What's one thing in your closet that you cannot live without?
3. What's one thing that most people probably don't know about you?
4. Name one thing that you want to do before you die.
5. What's one food that you cannot live without?
6. What quote/phrase do you live your life by?
7. What do you like and dislike about the YouTube community?
8. What's your number one most listened-to song on iTunes?
9. What kind of style would you define yourself as having?
10. What is your favorite number?
11. What are two of your hobbies?
12. What are two of your pet peeves?
13. What is one of your guilty pleasures?

THIS OR THAT BEAUTY TAG: This is one of the longest beauty tags out there, but the questions are super easy to answer, which also helps keep the video length down to a reasonable level!

1. Blush or bronzer?
2. Lip gloss or lipstick?
3. Eyeliner or mascara?
4. Foundation or concealer?
5. Neutral or color eye shadow?
6. Pressed or loose eye shadows?
7. Brushes or sponges?
8. OPI or China Glaze nail polish?
9. Long or short nails?
10. Acrylic or natural nails?
11. Bright or dark nail polish?
12. Nail art or plain?
13. Perfume or body splash?
14. Lotion or body butter?
15. Body wash or soap?
16. Lush or Bath & Body Works?
17. Jeans or sweatpants?
18. Long or short-sleeved shirts?
19. Dresses or skirts?
20. Stripes or plaids?
21. Flip-flops or sandals?
22. Scarves or hats?
23. Studs or dangly earrings?
24. Necklaces or bracelets?
25. Heels or flats?
26. Cowboy boots or riding boots?
27. Jacket or hoodie?
28. Forever 21 or Charlotte Russe?
29. Abercrombie or Hollister?
30. Saks 5th Avenue or Nordstrom?
31. Curly or straight hair?
32. Bun or ponytail?

33. Bobby pins or butterfly clips?
34. Hair spray or gel?
35. Long or short hair?
36. Light or dark hair?
37. Side swept bangs or full bangs?
38. Hair up or down?
39. Rain or shine?
40. Summer or winter?
41. Fall or spring?
42. Chocolate or vanilla?
43. East coast or West coast?

TMI TAG: This "too much information" tag is actually fairly innocent, and you can omit any questions you don't feel comfortable asking. This tag is rather long, so keep your answers short to ensure your video comes in around 15 minutes. If you really like to chat, you can always break this up into two different videos.

1. What are you wearing?
2. Ever been in love?
3. Ever had a terrible breakup?
4. How tall are you?
5. How much do you weigh?
6. Any tattoos?
7. Any piercings?
8. Favorite television show?
9. Favorite band?
10. Favorite song?
11. Someone you miss.
12. How old are you?
13. What's your Zodiac sign?
14. What quality do you look for in a partner?
15. Favorite quote?

16. Favorite actor?
17. Favorite color?
18. Loud music or soft?
19. Where do you go when you're sad?
20. How long does it take you to shower?
21. How long does it take you to get ready in the morning?
22. Ever been in a physical fight?
23. What's a turn-on for you?
24. What's a turn-off?
25. What is the reason you joined YouTube?
26. What are your fears?
27. Last thing that made you cry?
28. Last time you said you loved someone?
29. Meaning behind your YouTube name?
30. Last book you read?
31. The book you're currently reading.
32. Last television you watched?
33. Last person you talked to?
34. The relationship between you and the person you last texted.
35. Favorite food?
36. Place you want to visit?
37. Last place you were?
38. Do you have a crush?
39. Last time you kissed someone?
40. Last time you were insulted?
41. Favorite flavor of sweet?
42. What instruments, if any, do you play?
43. Favorite piece of jewelry?
44. Last sport you played?
45. Last song you sang?
46. Last time you hung out with anyone?
47. Who should answer these questions next?

12 CHRISTMAS QUESTIONS TAG: Holiday tags are best filmed at the start of the season. This is a very popular tag that you'll see popping up at the beginning of December with the questions being super-fast and easy to answer!

1. Favorite holiday colors?
2. Biggest holiday pet peeve?
3. Do you plan ahead or procrastinate?
4. How old were you when you stopped believing in Santa?
5. Favorite classic holiday song?
6. Favorite modern holiday song?
7. Favorite Christmas tradition?
8. Real or fake tree?
9. When do you put the Christmas tree up and take it down?
10. Favorite holiday cookie/treat?
11. What's at the top of your tree?
12. Do you decorate outside?
13. What did you always wish for but never got?

20 QUESTIONS TAG: Here's another get-to-know-you tag, although note that this one does lean towards girls and beauty.

1. Thing you cannot leave the house without.
2. Favorite brand of makeup?
3. Favorite flowers?
4. Favorite clothing stores?
5. Favorite perfume?
6. Heels or flats?
7. Do you or did you get good grades in school?
8. Favorite colors?
9. Do you drink energy drinks?
10. Do you drink juice?
11. Do you like swimming?

12. Do you eat fries with a fork?

13. What's your favorite moisturizer?

14. Are you or do you want to get married?

15. Do you get mad easily?

16. Are you into ghost hunting?

17. Any phobias?

18. Do you bite your nails?

19. Have you ever had a near-death experience?

20. Do you drink coffee?

20 QUESTIONS ABOUT MUSIC TAG: Another page, another music tag! The questions in this one, however, are straightforward to answer, making it a relatively quick video to film.

1. Which band or artist do you own the most albums by?

2. What was the last song you listened to?

3. What's in your CD player right now?

4. What was the last concert you attended?

5. What was the greatest concert you've ever been to?

6. What's the worst concert you've ever been to?

7. What's the most musically involved you have ever been?

8. What concert are you looking forward to?

9. What is your favorite band shirt?

10. What musician would you like to hang out with for a day?

11. Who is one musician or group you wish would make a comeback?

12. Who is one band or artist you've never seen live but always wanted to?

13. Name four or more flawless albums.

14. How many music-related videos or DVDs do you own?

15. How many concerts have you been to in total?

16. Who have you seen the most live?

17. What is your favorite movie soundtrack?

18. What was your last musical "phase" before you wizened up?
19. What's your "guilty music pleasure" that you hate to admit to liking?

20 QUESTIONS MOMMY TAG: While many YouTube tags were developed by the teenage set, here's a great tag just for moms online! Any mommy can answer these questions regardless of how old their child is.

1. Are you a stay-at-home or work-outside-the-home mom?
2. Would you have it any other way?
3. Do you co-sleep?
4. One must-have gear for baby?
5. How many kids do you plan on having?
6. Do you do date nights with your husband? If so, how many per month?
7. Your child's favorite TV show?
8. Name one thing you bought before you had your baby but never ended up using.
9. Your child's favorite food?
10. How many cars does your family have?
11. Weight gain before pregnancy, during, after, and now?
12. Dream vacation with your kiddos?
13. Dream vacation without the kiddos?
14. How has your life changed since your baby has been born?
15. Finish the sentence, "It makes my heart melt to see..."
16. Where do you shop for your kids' clothing?
17. Favorite mommy make-up and skin care products?
18. Huggies Diaper Jeans: Yay or Nay?
19. Have you always wanted kids?
20. Best part about being a mom?

21 HAIR QUESTIONS TAG: Finally, a tag that isn't about makeup....instead, it's all about hair, haha! Makeup, skincare, and hair styling are all very popular video topics on YouTube, so if beauty is your thing, don't hesitate to jump right in!

1. Why did you start taking better care of your hair?
2. What are your two favorite hair products?
3. Whose hair did you admire as a child?
4. What is your ultimate goal length?
5. How are you going to celebrate when you reach your ultimate goal length?
6. Two styles you want to try at your goal length.
7. Which do you prefer: health or length?
8. Which do you prefer: hair times with no metal parts or butterfly clips?
9. What products do you prefer: salon brands, organic brands, or drugstore brands?
10. Which product or technique do you think is overrated?
11. Which product/technique do you think is under-rated?
12. What is your favorite part of your hair regimen?
13. What is the most annoying part of your hair regimen?
14. Oils or Butters?
15. Buns or Ponytails?
16. Wigs or Weaves?
17. What is your opinion of growth aids?
18. At what length do you consider hair long?
19. When was the last time you visited a salon?
20. What types of hair information do you pursue most often online: YouTube videos, blogs, or discussion forums?
21. And finally, what piece of advice would you give to someone just starting out on their hair journey?

22 LIFE QUESTIONS TAG: This tag offers lots of thought-provoking questions, but be careful about rambling on, or else your video will quickly balloon to an hour long! YouTube really prefers videos that are 10-15 minutes in length, so keep that in mind when filming and editing.

1. How old would you be if you didn't know how old you were?
2. If life is so short, why do we do so many things we don't like and like so many things we don't do?
3. What is the one thing you'd most like to change about the world?
4. If the average human life span was 40 years, how would you live your life differently?
5. Are you more worried about doing things right or doing the right things?
6. If you could offer a newborn child only one piece of advice, what would it be?
7. Would you break the law to save a loved one?
8. What's something you know you do differently than most people?
9. What one thing have you not done that you really want to do? What's holding you back?
10. Are you holding onto something you need to let go of?
11. If you had to move to a state or country besides the one you currently live in, where would it be and why?
12. Which is worse, when a good friend moves away or loses touch with a good friend who lives right by you?
13. What are you most grateful for?
14. Would you rather lose all of your old memories or never be able to make new ones?
15. Has your greatest fear ever come true?
16. Do you remember that time 5 years ago when you were

extremely upset? Does it really matter now?

17. What is your happiest childhood memory?
18. Have you ever been with someone, said nothing, and walked away feeling like you just had the best conversation ever?
19. If you just won a million dollars, would you quit your job?
20. What is the difference between being alive and truly living?
21. What would you do differently if you knew nobody would judge you?
22. Decisions are being made right now. The question is: are you making them for yourself or are you letting others make them for you?

THE TWILIGHT SAGA TAG: Bella and Edward...or Bella and Jacob? If you have a strong opinion about the "Twilight" books and movies, this is the tag for you!

1. Which book in the series is your favorite?
2. How long did it take you to read the books?
3. Who introduced you to the books?
4. What's your dream ending to the series?
5. Who is your favorite vampire?
6. Who is your favorite werewolf?
7. What is one of your favorite quotes from the books?
8. What was your favorite Bella/Edward moment?
9. What was your favorite Bella/Jacob moment?
10. Which book cover was your favorite?
11. Who do you want to see Bella with most, Edward or Jacob?
12. Have you watched all of the movies?
13. Did you see the movies in the theatre or on video?
14. Do you own all of the movies on DVD or Blu-ray?
15. Who were your favorite actors in the movies?
16. Which actors did you not like?
17. In which book did you like Bella best?

18. In which book did you like Edward best?
19. In which book did you like Jacob best?
20. Which actor would you most like to meet?

THE TWIN TAG: Use your twin power to film this fun tag video! If you both have YouTube channels, each of you can film a video interviewing the other one and then cross-promote the videos on each other's channels!

1. Who is the oldest?
2. Can you show an old photo of the two of you together?
3. Favorite memory together?
4. Each other's dream jobs?
5. Who takes longer to get ready in the morning?
6. Do you have anything matching?
7. Did you ever dress alike?
8. Song you would use to describe each other.
9. What color are your auras?
10. One thing that you can do well that the other can't.
11. Do you have the same personalities?
12. Silliest question about being twins?
13. Describe each other in one word.
14. One thing that annoys you about each other?
15. If you could go anywhere in the world together, where would it be and why?
16. Nicknames you have for each other
17. What do you order at fast food restaurants?
18. Favorite thing about each other?
19. Favorite inside joke?
20. Are you identical or fraternal twins?

WINTERLICIOUS TAG: Here's the final seasonal tag in this book, and once again, some of the questions are beauty-related. However, feel free to omit any questions that don't apply to you and/or add any others you think up!

1. Favorite winter nail polish?
2. Favorite winter lip product?
3. Most worn winter clothing piece?
4. Most worn winter accessory?
5. Favorite winter scent or candle?
6. Favorite winter beverage?
7. All-time favorite Christmas or holiday movie?
8. Favorite holiday song?
9. Favorite holiday food or treat?
10. What is your favorite Christmas decoration this year?
11. What's at the top of your wish list?
12. What are your plans for the holidays this year?

THE WOULD YOU RATHER BEAUTY TAG #1: This is the first of TWO would-you-rather beauty tags. I suggest either filming but spacing them out OUR combining your favorite questions from each into one video.

1. Would you rather go out with messy hair and nice make-up OR nice hair and no make-up?
2. Would you rather shave your eyebrows OR have your eyelashes fall out?
3. Would you rather be forced to shop at only MAC OR Sephora for the rest of your life?
4. Would you rather wear lip gloss and lip liner OR an 80's perm?
5. Would you rather leave the house with an obvious foundation line OR an overdone blush?
6. Would you rather wear MC Hammer pants OR biker shorts in public?

7. Would you rather have a bad orange spray tan OR really weird tan lines that can't be covered?
8. Would you rather have a bad haircut OR a bad hair color?
9. Would you rather have YouTube OR Twitter taken away forever/
10. Would you rather give up using makeup brushes OR mascara?

THE WOULD YOU RATHER BEAUTY TAG #2: Finally, the very last beauty tag in this book! This one is an extension of the one before; as I said, you can film each separately or edit the questions to combine them into a single video.

1. Would you rather walk around all day with your skirt tucked into your underwear OR be seen wearing a really see-through dress?
2. Would you rather go to a party and not realize until the end of the night that you have lipstick on your teeth OR that your fake lashes were coming unglued?
3. Would you rather forget to put mascara on one eye OR forget blush on one side of your face?
4. Would you rather wear a lipstick and lip liner combo OR a frosty blue eye shadow?
5. Would you rather wear a foundation that is two shades too light OR go way overboard on bronzer?
6. Would you rather drink an entire bottle of ketchup OR run into the guy who broke your heart on a bad hair day with your skin breaking out?
7. Would you rather be able to date any celebrity you wanted OR wake up with perfect red carpet-worthy hair?
8. Would you rather your armpits smell musky or like delicious lasagna?
9. Would you rather give up your make-up OR your cell phone

for one year?

10. Would you rather run into a cute guy you like with food stuck in your teeth OR wearing no make-up at all?

THE WOULD YOU RATHER TAG: This is a very long tag with questions that lead to long answers. My suggestion is to either pick out your favorite questions or break this one up into two separate videos.

1. Would you rather live in a world where you rule OR live in a world with no problems?
2. Would you rather always take a cold shower OR sleep an hour less than you need to be fully rested?
3. Would you rather always have to say everything on your mind OR never speak again?
4. Would you rather lose OR never play?
5. Would you rather always wear earmuffs OR a nose plug?
6. Would you rather be 3 feet tall OR 8 feet tall?
7. Would you rather be a dog named Killer OR a cat named Fluffy?
8. Would you rather be a giant hamster OR a tiny rhino?
9. Would you rather be able to hear any conversation OR take back anything you say?
10. Would you rather be able to read everyone's mind all of the time OR always know their future?
11. Would you rather be able to stop time OR fly?
12. Would you rather be born with an elephant truck OR a giraffe neck?
13. Would you rather be forced to tell your best friend a lie OR your parents the truth?
14. Would you rather be forgotten OR hatefully remembered?
15. Would you rather go about your normal day naked OR fall asleep for a year?
16. Would you rather be gossiped about OR never talked about

at all?

17. Would you rather be hairy all over OR completely bald?
18. Would you rather be happy for 8 hours a day and poor OR sad for 8 hours a day and rich?
19. Would you rather be invisible OR be able to read minds?
20. Would you rather be rich and ugly OR poor and good-looking?
21. Would you rather be stranded on an island alone OR with someone you hate?
22. Would you rather be the most popular OR the smartest person you know?
23. Would you rather eat a bar of soap OR drink a bottle of dishwashing liquid?
24. Would you rather eat a handful of hair OR lick three public telephones?
25. Would you rather eat a tub of BUTTER OR a gallon of ice cream?
26. Would you rather eat a tub of margarine OR 5 tablespoons of hot pepper sauce?
27. Would you rather eat poison ivy OR a handful of bumblebees?
28. Would you rather end hunger OR hatred?
29. Would you rather find true love OR 10 million dollars?
30. Would you rather forget who you were OR who everyone else was?
31. Would you rather give bad advice OR take bad advice?
32. Would you rather give up your computer OR your pet?
33. Would you rather go to an amusement park OR a family reunion?
34. Would you rather go without television OR junk food for the rest of your life?
35. Would you rather have a beautiful house and an ugly car OR

an ugly house and a beautiful car?

36. Would you rather have a kangaroo OR koala as your pet?
37. Would you rather have a missing finger OR have an extra toe?
38. Would you rather have one wish granted today OR three wishes granted in 10 years?
39. Would you rather have X-ray vision OR bionic hearing?
40. Would you rather kiss a jellyfish OR step on a crab?
41. Would you rather know it all OR have it all?
42. Would you rather live without music OR television?
43. Would you rather love but not be loved back OR be loved but never love in return?
44. Would you rather never use the internet again OR never watch television again/
45. Would you rather only be able to whisper OR only be able to shout?
46. Would you rather own a ski lodge OR a surf camp?
47. Would you rather publish your diary OR make a movie about your most embarrassing moment?
48. Would you rather spend all day surfing the internet OR the ocean?

ZOMBIE APOCALYPSE TAG: It is somewhat appropriate that the final tag in this section relates to the potential end of the world!

1. Which three YouTubers would you have in your team?
2. The object immediately to your left is your only weapon – what is it?
3. If you were a zombie, who would you want to bite?
4. What would your survival plan be?
5. What would you do if your parents became zombies?
6. Do you want the zombie apocalypse to happen?

CONCLUSION

With just a camera or smartphone, a computer, and an internet connection, anyone can start a YouTube channel. However, it takes commitment and perseverance to grow an audience and make MONEY on the site. While a handful of people have gotten rich over the years by making videos, for most people, YouTube offers a bit of extra spending money, perhaps even enough to qualify it as a part-time job. How much you earn is up to you regarding how much time and effort you are willing to put into producing quality content that viewers respond to.

Putting yourself out there in front of thousands and potentially millions of people is a scary proposition. However, if you approach YouTube for your own personal enjoyment and growth before anything else, you will have a successful channel that also brings you some income.

YouTube can be stressful. Dealing with negative comments, having to redo videos, and navigating through technical difficulties can all take their toll. The good thing is that your YouTube channel is YOURS. You can put up as many videos as you want or as few as you want. Need a break? Take it! Step away for a few days, a week, or even a month. Yes, consistency is rewarded on YouTube, but not at the expense of your mental health.

Start your YouTube channel for fun. And at the beginning, just focus on having a good time with your channel. There is no need to worry about the social media stuff and back-end work. Just get some videos up to get your feet wet. No one likes the first videos they film, and that is okay. Forgetting to look directly into the camera, realizing you have a stain on your shirt, mispronouncing words....it all comes with the territory.

Practice does make perfect when it comes to running a YouTube channel. Trust me the more videos you film, the more comfortable you will become. You will find your footing and your voice. And you will find your audience. There are people out there just wanting the type of content you will produce. With consistency, they will find you.

There will be times when you want to quit, but I urge you to just stick with it. It can be hard at the beginning when you aren't yet monetized, but once you hit 1,000 subscribers and have 4,000 watch hours, you will start to earn money on your videos. And being paid for your work is even more rewarding.

With all the work involved, why do I make YouTube videos? After all, it's not a full-time job for me. I've had many ups and downs on the site. I've cried over mean comments. I've been jealous when other creators blew past me with their subscriber counts. And I've been so discouraged that I just wanted to delete every video I ever filmed.

But no matter how frustrated I've gotten with YouTube over the years, I always return to the platform. After all, most of my online "friends" are fellow creators. I have a small community of like-minded entrepreneurs on the site who always have my back no matter what I do.

At the end of the day, YouTube is just plain FUN! I've filmed everything from baking videos to Walt Disney World vacation vlogs. I've gotten tons of free products from brands. I have videos of the days I brought my two dogs home. I have thousands of hours of professional and personal footage of my life that I can look back on at any time.

And the money can be good. Whether it is from Google AdSense directly or from the sale of my products, YouTube has been a huge part of my business success. I don't think I would have sold near the number of books I have over the years had my YouTube viewers not been the first ones to buy them. My subscribers have also been my first Etsy customers, enabling me to open a second shop.

YouTube is now woven into my daily life. Even on days when I'm not filming or uploading, I'm still checking my channel and replying to comments. The customer base I've cultivated on YouTube is a big part of my self-employment success. I can't imagine giving it up!

And as for YOU: If you haven't already started a YouTube channel, I hope this book has inspired you to take the leap. And if you already have a channel but are struggling, just know I've been there, too. YouTube is, after all, a business. It's a job. Jobs can be fun. But they can also be hard.

But with YouTube, YOU are your own boss. You set your own hours and your own rules. Stay true to yourself and create the content you are passionate about. The views, the subscribers, and the money will come in time. But more importantly, you will gain confidence in having built up something that is uniquely yours!

OTHER BOOKS BY ANN ECKHART

Are you interested in other ways you can make money online? Be sure to visit Ann Eckhart's Amazon Author Page at **https://amzn.to/3wBF0WF** for all of her business books, including:

- **Beginner's Guide To Selling On eBay**
- **Beginner's Guide To Amazon KDP**
- **Beginner's Guide To Selling On Whatnot**
- **Beginner's Guide To Selling Antiques on Etsy**
- **Beginner's Guide To Selling Crafts on Etsy**
- **Beginner's Guide To Starting An Etsy Sticker Shop**
- **Beginner's Guide To Starting An Etsy Print-On-Demand Shop**
- **Beginner's Guide To Selling Digital Products on Etsy**
- **101 Items To Sell On eBay**
- **101 More Items To Sell On eBay**

ABOUT THE AUTHOR

Ann Eckhart is a writer, entrepreneur, and online content creator based in Iowa. She has written numerous books about how to make money online from home. For all of her books, visit her Amazon Author Page at: https://amzn.to/3wBF0WF

You can also follow Ann Eckhart on these social media sites:

FACEBOOK: https://www.facebook.com/anneckhart/

TWITTER: https://twitter.com/ann_eckhart

INSTAGRAM: https://instagram.com/ann_marie_eckhart

YOUTUBE: https://tinyurl.com/yxvqtwc7

COPYRIGHT 2023 Ann Eckhart

No part of this book may be reprinted or reproduced without express written permission from the author.

Cover Design by Ann Eckhart

Don't miss out!

Visit the website below and you can sign up to receive emails whenever Ann Eckhart publishes a new book. There's no charge and no obligation.

https://books2read.com/r/B-A-UQFB-ZOBTC

BOOKS 2 READ

Connecting independent readers to independent writers.

Also by Ann Eckhart

101 Items To Sell On Ebay
101 Items To Sell On Ebay
101 More Items To Sell On Ebay

2022 Home Based Business Books
Beginner's Guide To Amazon KDP 2022 Edition: How To Create &
Sell Books Using Kindle Direct Publishing
Beginner's Guide To Selling On Ebay 2022 Edition: How To Start &
Grow a Successful Online Reselling Business from Home
Beginner's Guide To YouTube 2022 Edition: How To Start & Grow a
Successful & Profitable YouTube Channel

2023 Home Based Business Books
Beginner's Guide To Selling On Ebay: 2023 Edition

Standalone
2020 Ebay Sourcing Guide
Ebay Seller Secrets

How to Start a YouTube Channel for Fun & Profit

Beginner's Guide To Amazon KDP: 2023 Edition

Beginner's Guide To Starting An Etsy Print-On-Demand Shop

Beginner's Guide To Starting An Etsy Sticker Shop

Beginner's Guide To WhatNot: How To Buy & Sell On The Live Auction Reselling App

Reseller Liquidation Database: The Top 35 Liquidation & Wholesale Companies for Online Sellers

2000+ Printable Products To Sell On Etsy

Beginner's Guide To Selling Digital Products On Etsy

Beginner's Guide To Amazon KDP 2024 Edition

Beginner's Guide To Selling Antiques On Etsy

Beginner's Guide To Selling Crafts On Etsy

Beginner's Guide To Selling On eBay 2024 Edition

Beginner's Guide To Starting a YouTube Channel 2024-2025 Edition

Watch for more at www.SeeAnnSave.com.

www.ingramcontent.com/pod-product-compliance
Lightning Source LLC
Chambersburg PA
CBHW061434150726
47987CB00001B/207